HOLY SPIRIT

OTHER BOOKS BY MICHAEL KOULIANOS

The Jesus Book

Jesus 365

Healing Presence

HOLY SPIRIT

THE ONE WHO MAKES JESUS REAL

MICHAEL KOULIANOS

DESTINY IMAGE® PUBLISHERS, INC.

P.O. Box 310, Shippensburg, PA 17257-0310

"Promoting Inspired Lives."

This book and all other Destiny Image and Destiny Image Fiction books are available at Christian bookstores and distributors worldwide.

Cover design by Eileen Rockwell
Interior design by Terry Clifton

For more information on foreign distributors, call 717-532-3040.

Or reach us on the Internet: www.destinyimage.com

ISBN 13 TP: 978-0-7684-1168-3
ISBN 13 EBook: 978-0-7684-1169-0
LP ISBN: 978-0-7684-1537-7
HC ISBN: 978-0-7684-1536-0

For Worldwide Distribution, Printed in the U.S.A.
1 2 3 4 5 6 / 20 19 18 17

First and foremost, this book is dedicated to the Holy Spirit. You are the One who makes Jesus real to me.

To my wife, Jessica, who I love more than words can explain.

To my children, Benny, Theo, and Sofia, you will carry on this message and power of the Holy Spirit to the world for the rest of your lives. The nations are crying out for the reality of Jesus. This only comes by His Spirit. Walk in the presence and power of God in your generation. I love you and believe in you more than you know. You can do it. I know you can.

CONTENTS

FOREWORD
BY BILL JOHNSON

In recent years, Michael and Jessica Koulianos have become personal friends of mine. This has been a great privilege and joy for me, as they are amazing and very real people. I have loved seeing how the message they've declared from the pulpit is lived out when the crowds are gone. I've also enjoyed watching them put absolute trust in God when they've faced some pretty rough situations. The idea of surrendering all to Jesus is not just a good idea; it is their reality—and wonderfully so. Truth must go beyond concepts and principles and go deep into the heart so it can be measured. And the most practical place to see the impact of truth upon a life is in one's relationships. Of all the relationships that matter, family is first. They have done family so well.

Authenticity is one of the primary things I look for in a person who stands in a pulpit declaring what God is saying. It's important for me to know whether they preach ideals they've not yet practiced or whether they speak from their own experience. It's not that I'd find fault with or accuse those who aren't quite what they teach, as we all see things that are beyond our own experience. It's just important for me to know what has been proven through the test of a life lived well and what remains an unproven idea. Authenticity is one of the building blocks of trust in ministry. And it's a joy to say this family is genuine and trustworthy.

One of the other things I look for in a person's life is joy. This has become more and more important to me as I get older. My own weakness in my early years has made this a personal priority. I certainly knew joy and enjoyed so many of the blessings in Christ. But I also knew too well how to be intense, often draining the joy out of the delightful journey of following Jesus. Perhaps the greatest feature of the author and his family is this quality—*joy!* They know how to enjoy family, friends, ministry, and life itself, celebrating the goodness of God throughout the journey. It's beautiful to watch. From a life lived well, Michael has written what will ignite the hearts of many, encouraging them to draw near to God at any price. *Holy Spirit* is a tool that God will use to transform many lives.

The following pages are rich in history, brilliant in practical insights, and filled with a whole bunch of inspiration for anyone who hungers for more of God. Many years ago, Michael said "yes" to an invitation given by the Holy Spirit Himself. This book is the product of the journey that came from that "yes." He writes with authority because it comes from his own fruitful experience. He discovered that to follow Jesus well, we have to become sensitive to the Holy Spirit, for Jesus is Lord of our life only to the measure that we respond to the leadings of the Holy Spirit.

Throughout this book, the author gives us compelling reasons to live a life full of the Holy Spirit. And while in this kind of life we find out who we are and how God wants to use us, the real prize is

God Himself. We all want to be used by God to affect humanity. We all desire to impact the course of world history. But knowing God is the main thing, from which the rest of life is to flow.

The simple but profound conclusion is that life is all about Jesus. Michael came to realize and believe wholeheartedly that the Christian life is the life of Jesus in us and through us by the Holy Spirit. He speaks of the Bible as "much more than a book. It's an experience" and adds, "Did you know that the church fathers called the Holy Scriptures 'the book of experience'? But they were after something more. They were after the Person of the Bible. God gave us the Bible to bring us to Himself." I love this, and you will too.

Ready yourself to enjoy this encouraging and instructional book that will impact your own relationship with God, leading you to a more fulfilled life.

BILL JOHNSON
Bethel Church, Redding, CA
Author of *When Heaven Invades Earth*
and *God is Good*

Chapter One

HAVE YOU EVER SEEN JESUS?

It was a dark and gloomy night in Tarpon Springs, Florida, in 1984. My uncle had just passed away from cancer. The family had gathered in his wife's home for a meal and a time to remember his life. This is very common in my Greek culture. I vividly remember everyone wearing black to show their mourning. The house was packed—so packed there was no room to sit in the living room so I sat there on the floor, taking in the somber and tear-filled atmosphere. The women were serving the men their food, which is the way things are in our culture. There I was, sitting at my dad's feet. I felt safe there. My dad is a strong man—a military man with a law degree and a successful business. He is a man's man, raised in Gary, Indiana, which was one of the toughest and most dangerous cities in America at the time. I still remember hearing the wailing over my deceased uncle coming from the women. It was such a sad moment. Death has its way of lingering and permeating the lives of those who don't know Jesus. Its darkness is feared for that reason. Death can be felt.

Suddenly, there was a knock on the door. Through the door came a man wearing a priest's collar. When he walked into this home filled with sadness, everything changed in a moment! I mean everything. Our faces instantly changed from showing anguish to displaying attentiveness. The air was no longer heavy with hopelessness. It was literally filled with an invisible, cloudlike substance that seemed to have electric waves moving through it. My seven-year-old mind described the moment this way: "God just came into this room with this priest. This man is God's friend."

The priest's name was Anthony Morfessis. My family called him Father Anthony. He was no ordinary priest. I had grown up around clergy my entire life. Sadly, most were focused on orthodoxy rather than Jesus. But this man, well, he was a different breed altogether. His face was broken and piercing, supple and focused, determined yet dependent upon Another. His eyes were full of fire and love, all at once and all in one man. These beautiful qualities flow from only one person, Jesus. This man had Jesus, and I knew it. I vividly remember Father Anthony standing in the corner of the living room as he began to pray for the women in the home. They instantly began to cry and scream as they hit the floor when he touched them. I had never seen anything like it in my life. The electricity continued to fill the room. Little did I know that what I was feeling was not a "something," but a Someone. His name is the Holy Spirit.

Then the priest looked at my father, Theo, who was just days out of surgery. My earliest memories of my dad are of a strong and healthy man who was a tireless worker. Then he contracted a disease called aquarium granuloma, which put him in a wheelchair or on crutches for much of the time in those days. This rare disease attacked the tissue and bone in his left knee. It had entered his system through a scratch on his knee. The bacteria came from sponges, coral, or shells. My parents had a thriving gift shop and tourism business in my hometown of Tarpon Springs. It is a predominantly Greek community on the Gulf of Mexico. Mom and Dad were blessed to have their businesses. Dad was a hard worker. He loved to handle the sponges and coral himself. One day, out of nowhere, the infection entered his system. The infection from the disease was so bad that they put him on two thousand milligrams of tetracycline a day for five years. This wrecked his stomach and digestive system. Even though I was very young at the time, I have vivid memories of Dad with drainage tubes, in a wheelchair, or on crutches.

As my dad sat on the couch with our mourning family surrounding him, the priest sat down across the room and began to stare at my father. Then, the Spirit-filled man of God boldly asked my dad a question that would frame and change my life forever. He said, "Have you ever seen Jesus?" Wow! What a question. My father replied, "No, Father, I haven't." Father Anthony responded, "Why not?" A bit confused and frustrated, my dad said, "I don't know." The priest asked, "Do you want to?" I couldn't believe my ears! This was going to be amazing. This was not your average memorial service. To my seven-year-old mind, this could only mean one thing: Jesus was going to appear right in the middle of my cousins' living room—maybe something like out of *Star Trek*. We would all see Him visibly for just a moment. "What a night this will be!" To everyone's shock, rather than Jesus appearing before our eyes, Father Anthony stood up and began to walk toward my father. Remember, he had no idea my dad was just out of surgery. Nor did he know that there were crutches behind the couch. Nor did he know anything about my dad's disease. On the other hand, maybe Someone told him. Maybe he could hear from Someone who we did not know at the time. Perhaps Father Anthony had secret information straight from Heaven. Was he a friend of the One we were feeling like electricity in the room? With fire in his eyes and boldness in each step, Father Anthony locked onto my dad's leg and made a straight line to him. Immediately, he gripped Dad's knee in his hand. It was the exact knee that had been operated on a couple days before. You have to understand, my dad was wearing long pants. There was nothing pointing to my dad's disease. For all Father Anthony knew, my dad was just a guy sitting on a couch, paying his respects to a family member who had passed away. As you can imagine, my father jerked with pain as the bold priest began to take hold of the incision that was kept together with staples in Dad's flesh. What in the world was happening? I thought we were going to see Jesus.

You have to understand, the entire scene was foreign to me. First of all, nobody messed with my dad. He was a military man. A strong ethnic man. His favorite movies are *Rambo* and *Rocky*. That should help give you a mental picture of my dad. Well, back to the story. All of a sudden, the pain turned into fire, and it shot through Dad's body. The same power that filled the house began to flow through Dad's leg. Father Anthony then spoke these words with absolute authority: "In the name of Jesus Christ of Nazareth, I command you to walk." So, Dad stood up, reached behind the couch to grab his crutches, and was going to attempt to walk with them. The priest said, "No crutches! Walk in Jesus' name." So, Dad took a step, and the fiery electricity continued to flow through his leg. Then, another and another. The tears flowed down Dad's face as God healed him. This was my first experience with a miracle, and a miracle it was!

A day or two later, my father went to see the orthopedic surgeon who had operated on him. Even though I was only seven years old at the time, I remember going with him to this appointment. Part of Dad's exam was to do a strength test. As the doctor looked on, Dad pressed more firmly with his left leg—the one that had been operated on—than he did with his good leg! To add to the surgeon's shock, when he began to examine Dad's left leg, he discovered that all the muscle that had atrophied in Dad's thigh over the last five years had grown back as hard as a rock overnight! Dad was healed.

What power healed my father? Who was causing the heat in his leg? Who had filled the room with such a tangible substance that I haven't forgotten it thirty-one years later? Who crashed into our lives when we knew absolutely nothing about Him? Who could be so loving? He is the Holy Spirit.

And now, I pray that He will introduce Himself to you. I hear you asking, "How will I know when I meet Him?" Trust me, you will know. There is nobody like Him.

Chapter Two

HE CAME FOR ME

It was a warm Orlando afternoon in 1989. After driving three hours from Tarpon Springs, my mother, brother, other family and friends, and I turned left from Forest City Road into the parking lot of the Orlando Christian Center. Immediately, I felt something on my body and deep within me. It was a deep hunger and anticipation that flooded my being. I knew God was on this property, and I had to meet Him. I was withered down and weakened after six months of mononucleosis that had become Epstein-Barr disease. I was unable to attend school and do the things that a typical twelve-year-old boy did with his time. But this moment was different. I knew God had something for me. I knew He was calling me. Everything I had ever wanted seemed to live in the atmosphere I was feeling on this church property.

To my surprise, there were hundreds of people already waiting to get into the service we were attending. Doors opened at 6:00 P.M. and many had been waiting since 2:00 P.M. This was not a promoted stadium event or conference. It was just a Sunday night healing service in a church. So, we all squeezed into the line. The people were so happy and expectant. They were singing worship songs that I had never heard, but they were beautiful. This scene was a shock to my system. I had grown up in a very faithful Greek Orthodox home. My cousin was a priest. Two other cousins were archbishops. My father was on the board of the local Greek Orthodox church we attended. I was faithful in Sunday school and was an altar boy. I was in church more than most of my friends and family members. But this was a different and miraculous scene. Never had I seen hundreds of people lining up to get into church! In fact, as a boy, I couldn't wait for church to end. These people were eagerly awaiting the moment the usher would open the doors so that they could be with Jesus...the Jesus I had heard about growing up. They seemed to yearn for His reality, and I was feeling the same.

The powerful and electric Presence continued to touch and surround us. One thing was for certain: the moment those doors opened, I knew I had to run—and run fast—to get us a seat. After waiting for what seemed like forever, the ushers opened the doors, and I sprinted down the center aisle of this strange-looking church. I bumped into many people, but I did not care. I knew God was present. I could feel Him all over me. The moment I crossed the doorway of the church, I knew I had stepped into a different world. The air was different. It was crisp and full of light. There was no fear or weariness. I could breathe easily and smiled from ear to ear. The people, young and old, were like little children. There was absolutely no other place in the world I would rather have been. It was as if I had stepped into Heaven. In a way, I had.

Finally, we found a seat close to the front on the left side of the platform. Talk about a rush! Once we were seated, the expectancy level was rising all over this church that had no icons, chandeliers, or incense. This was strange to me. What it did have, however, was what I had always been searching for...the Holy Spirit. After waiting for over another hour, one of the assistant pastors took the stage and opened the service in prayer. I'll never forget the huge smile on his face. This man was full of joy. The waves of power that were going through me only increased as he lead us in prayer. I was completely full of peace, expectancy, and love. My mind was at ease, but I felt my spirit longing for what was about to happen that night.

Following the opening prayer, a choir of eighty people were in position in the choir loft, which was overshadowed by the baptismal tank that hung above it. Immediately, Bruce Hughes began to play a solo on the piano, and I had never heard anything like it in my life. This was not mere music; it seemed to come from Heaven and find its way into my young heart. People began to shout and lift their hands without anyone directing them to do so. Then, the choir began to sing, and I instantly jumped to my feet and lifted my hands and joined them. It felt completely right and natural to praise God this way even though I had never been around worship like this. As we started to sing the old hymns, the power I had been feeling grew stronger and stronger. I was completely immersed in the experience. I had closed my eyes and was singing directly to Jesus. In that moment, nothing else mattered to me. In fact, nothing else existed. It was as if I had a direct and personal audience with Jesus Himself. It was glorious and beyond description.

After about fifteen minutes of worship, my eyes were still closed but the room changed instantaneously. As if the atmosphere could become more heavenly, it actually did. My twelve-year-old heart interpreted the moment this way: "The Holy Spirit just walked into this room, and He came in with someone who knew Him well." I mean, that's the only way to walk closely with a person, right? You have to know him, and he has to know you. I opened my eyes, and as I expected, someone had entered the room. I saw a man wearing an off-white suit, hair combed sharply to the side, who spoke with a very distinct accent. As he joined us in worship, it became immediately apparent that he knew God and God knew him. The ecstatic joy that filled my being was completely supernatural. I felt like I would explode with the beauty of God's presence. My cousin told me this pastor had grown up like I had, in the Greek Orthodox Church. I had heard that his father was Greek, like my family. I felt comfortable even though the scene was completely different than anything I had ever been around. One thing was undeniable—he knew Jesus, and I wanted to know Him too.

As the pastor, Benny Hinn, continued to lead us in worship, I noticed a lady behind me who had a red rash on her arms. Minutes later, I looked back at her, and the rash had completely disappeared. This was a full-blown miracle that I saw with my own eyes. I heard another sound that scared the daylights out of me. It was the eeriest shrieking sound I had ever heard. I asked my family, "What is that horrible noise?" One of them answered, "It's the sound of a demon leaving someone." Talk about pandemonium! Miracles, deliverances, glorious waves going through me...all within minutes of each other.

I will never forget Benny's message about coming to Jesus. He spoke of Jesus like he actually knew Him, not like the historical figure that I had grown up hearing about. With piercing eyes, He looked at the crowd and said, "Jesus is real. If you want Him, get down here." I jumped over everything in my way and ran down to the altar as though my world depended on it. All of the sudden, he said, "Young boy, get up here." My next memory is standing before him on the platform. As amazing as this was, I knew it was supposed to happen. The thick electric Presence was even stronger on the stage than it was in the crowd. As Pastor Benny took a step toward me, I felt a wave of heat and thickness go through me. My next memory is being on the floor, unable to move. Wave after wave of power flowed through my body. I couldn't get up for all the money in the world. I could hear everything around me, yet at the same time, I felt like I was in Heaven. I didn't want this to end. It was absolutely the most wonderful feeling I have ever had. The person of the Holy Spirit had actually come to meet me. A young, bashful Greek kid was being touched personally by the God of the universe. It meant the world to me.

Benny then prayed for my brother and my mom. I heard his distinct Middle Eastern accent in a faded, echoic tone, even though he was only a few feet away from me. He said, "This young boy is mightily anointed. God will use him to touch the world. He has a great calling. Pick him up again." Instantly, two huge guys in suits picked me up and set me on my feet. Again, Pastor Benny moved toward me, and a mighty wind-like heat overwhelmed my body and I hit the floor. I began to tremble and shake. Pastor Benny repeatedly said, "God is anointing this young boy." I had no clue what his prophetic word meant. I had never been exposed to phrases like those. But I was certain that my life was changing and my destiny was being set in motion. While other kids were playing with their friends and pursuing what a typical child enjoys, this atmosphere became home and my all in all. I knew that this presence— the presence of the Holy Spirit—would become my life's ambition.

Finally, the same large men picked me up off the floor. People were beginning to leave. I wondered to myself, "What was that? What just happened to me? It has to continue. I never want to lose this feeling." Amazingly, my weakness and every symptom of the Epstein-Barr virus was gone! So gone that I never had to think about it again. To this day, I have never had a single symptom. What blew me away was that I knew Jesus was living in my heart. I could feel Him there. Everything changed that night in Orlando. My friend, everything can change for you as you read this book. My prayer is that within these pages, you will discover the same Person who saved, healed, and touched me—the Holy Spirit. Now, I want to share Him with you.

As I look back on my life and see all that God has done, the thousands or possibly millions who have been saved, healed, and touched by the Holy Spirit through our ministry, I hear the words of Benny that were spoken over me. They made no sense at the time. They actually seemed impossible in so many ways. I was well aware of all my weaknesses in the natural as a kid. Yes, I was a great athlete and good student. Those giftings were going to help me in the healing ministry very much. I was so shy in those days. My greatest fear was public speaking. I didn't enjoy speaking to people I didn't know. I didn't like being looked at. Speaking in front of my class at school was a nightmare to me. I'm telling you, I hated the thought of being the center of attention and having to address people. My two greatest passions growing up were golf and fishing. Neither of these required people! On paper, according to natural ability, I am the least qualified to preach the Gospel. My friend, I have learned something: Jesus doesn't care about our qualifications. As a great person once said, "He does not call the qualified; He qualifies the called." What is the qualification from Heaven's point of view? You got it. It's plain and simple: Have you been filled and clothed with the Holy Spirit? I believe that had I "earned" the ministry with natural ability, I would be tempted to point to myself in times of success. I am well aware of the fact that the boy who shook under the power of God for hours on the Orlando Christian Center floor was completely unlikely to succeed in the ministry according to the world's standards. What the world does not understand is that the Holy Spirit loves taking the unlikely and giving them His power instead of our own. This way, He is forever glorified. Today, as I stand on platforms and see the crowds, I know one thing for certain: it's all Him. He has done great things. I often say, "Jesus, thanks for the privilege. You are everything." Now more than ever, I believe the following verse: "'It is not by might. It is not by power. It is by My Spirit,' says the Lord of hosts." (see Zech. 4:6).

So today, I stand on the shoulders of those who have paid a price. I simply yield into those prophetic words spoken over me. I am praying for God's grace to carry on the power of the Spirit to a generation who often chooses natural gifting over a surrendered life. The world needs you to yield your life to God. Jesus is waiting to take your weaknesses and use them as trophies for His glory. When the Holy Spirit comes on you, you will become a different man or woman, just like King Saul did. That which frightened you, you will attack. Your limitation will dissolve into springboards that catapult you into your destiny. Mountains of fear will flatten before the Holy Spirit's touch on your life. At the end of the day, know this my friend: when you get Him, you get everything. You need nothing but God because every other need is found in Him. This is your moment. This is your time.

I believe He will touch you as you read this book. Maybe He will come into your car or visit you while you work. Maybe your encounter will come while you are praying. I cannot tell you when the Holy Spirit will touch you, but I can tell you that He will answer your invitation if you truly want to meet Him. He will become your dearest friend, teacher, and comforter.

HE COMES IN LOVE

Well, needless to say, everything was completely different after that. I felt completely brand-new. I remember singing all the way home on the three-hour drive back to Tarpon Springs. I sang and sang and sang. I'm sure my voice was all over the map, but I could have cared less. Something deep had happened to me. Even the air around me felt different. The sky and the trees were more beautiful. I felt like I could fly.

After that, people began coming up to me, saying, "Young man, God has something very special for you. You realize that what happened to you is rare, right?" I didn't have a clue what they were talking about. I was so full of joy that I just smiled at them and kept loving on Jesus. I thought everyone had a similar encounter. Looking back at my life, I am so humbled by the fact that Jesus came to me in such a rare and beautiful way. My friend, the beauty about Him is that He will do the same for you if you open your heart to Him. It may not look exactly like my encounter, but it will be equally as special to you because "He does all things well" (see Mark 7:37).

Now I had a Heavenly Father who gave me a sense of eternal love and belonging. There is no replacing the experience of knowing God as our Heavenly Father. This changes everything. We are not loved more or less based on how much we accomplish. We are loved because our Father is love and we are His children. Moreover, Jesus had become my devotion and model. This could only be experienced with my new friend, the Holy Spirit. And have we ever become friends! Let me say, He is not just any friend. He is God Almighty. He calls the shots and leads the dance. Yes, He wants us to cooperate and work with Him, but life with Him is not a democracy. You know, I love it this way. I trust Him way more than I trust myself. So, after my encounter, the Holy Spirit began to speak to me and nudge my new heart. He began to say things like, "Michael, I miss you today. Why don't you quit what you're doing right now and spend time with Me?" Oh, my heart would leap inside me. "This is real! He is real. He is really, really, really real. The Holy Spirit is speaking with me and touching me. He is here, and He is here to stay."

This began a love affair with Him that would soon become an addiction to being alone with Him in my room. Back then, I had no clue what I was doing when I would go into my room to pray. I didn't have many books and hadn't attended any conferences on the subject. I certainly didn't know much about intimacy with God. But He sure did. I had nothing to work with but a hungry heart and my Bible. I can tell you, that's all you need to have glorious experiences with the Lord.

HE LOVES HIS WORD

The Word of God became much more to me than a mere holy history book. It became bread to my soul. I couldn't put the Bible down.

I read the whole New Testament in a week when I was only twelve years old. The best part is that I began with the Book of Revelation. I knew that it freaked most people out, but I wanted to know how the whole thing ended before I began on that path. Don't you love how kids think? I had opened the Bible before, but it was different now. It was as though the Holy Spirit would sit next me and teach me the Word. Actually, it's His Word. He is the author of the Bible after all (see 2 Tim. 3:16). Those precious moments felt like He was showing off His favorite book, His Book.

I had noticed that some of the "born-again Christians" liked to highlight the Bible verses they enjoyed. I thought to myself, "Well, these are the people who led me to Jesus and changed my life. I want to be like them." So, I began highlighting all the verses that jumped out at me. There was only one problem—it seemed like every verse jumped out at me. There seemed to be more passages highlighted than not in my Bible. Little did I know that my young mind was being cleansed and my heart was filling up with Bread from Heaven.

GET MY FAMILY, GOD

After hours of being with Jesus day after day, I felt like I was going to explode with the love of God and His power. I had to tell my family. I had no pulpit or organized ministry, but I had a fresh power that I knew had made me brand-new. So, I went over to my grandmother's house for some food. When a Greek kid is hungry, there is only one place to go—Yiayia's ("grandmother" in Greek). My grandmother, Theodora Liolios, was the life of the family. She could cook, clean, and spank all at once. Let me tell you, she was an expert at all three. Her slipper-throwing technique was All-Star status. Those slippers seemed to have infrared heat-seeking devices in them. We would run away from her, and the slippers would turn the corner and chase us down.

Her home had an open-door policy. We just walked in and out whenever we wanted. Friends and family made for consistent laughter and endless excuses to eat.

I sat down next to my aunt and was bursting with the Holy Spirit. I said to her, "You know, Auntie, you need to meet Jesus and give Him your life." "Why?" she replied. I answered, "Because you're a sinner, and if you don't meet Jesus, you'll stay a sinner and sinners go to hell." I wish you could have seen her face. In our culture, you don't speak that way to an elder, especially a family member. I can still picture her face today. My aunt said, "If you call me a sinner one more time, I'll slap your face." My response was quick and simple: "The Bible says that 'all have sinned,'" I said, "and that includes you!" Probably not the most loving approach and probably not the exact wording I would use to begin a conversation today. Nonetheless, I was speaking complete and utter truth. The point is that I was burning with a desire to tell people about Jesus, and that, my friend, is proof that you have met the Holy Spirit. As badly as I wanted my aunt to get saved that day, she didn't. My goal was not to get her to "repeat a prayer." My passion was to be obedient and faithful to the Voice that was speaking to me. You see, I was doing it with Him and for Him. This is the great secret to a real relationship with the Holy Spirit.

THE HOLY SPIRIT GETS MY DAD

As glorious as my life had become, some of my family thought I had lost my mind. My mom and brother, Theo, had come to Jesus and were filled with the Holy Spirit. So was my cousin, Theo Billiris. A few more aunts and uncles had also come to the Lord. But there was one tough man who absolutely refused to give his heart to Jesus. It was my dad. Yes, even though he was miraculously healed and touched by the Lord four years earlier, he wanted nothing to do with what was happening to us.

You see, as a Greek family, you are Greek Orthodox. Whether you like it or not, in our culture you attend the Orthodox church. In our community and family, any other expression of Christian worship is not considered "true." This perspective was engrained in us. As a twelve-year-old, I remember riding in a car with one of our priests soon after I met Jesus. I asked him this question: "Father, what about someone in China? Someone who doesn't know a thing about Orthodoxy but has met Jesus? What if they really love Jesus and have given Him their life. Let's say they die but never attended an Orthodox church because there weren't any to attend. What happens to that person when they die? Do they go to Heaven, Father?" His response was quick and to the point: "Orthodoxy is the truth." I am not at all saying that this is the perspective of all who are Orthodox. I can only say that this is most certainly the perspective of many I grew up around. This is only my personal experience.

Let me say I absolutely love the Orthodox tradition. My personal library is full of the writings of the saints of the Orthodox Church. There is such a rich revelation on prayer and holiness. I so enjoy the Orthodox communion. The symbolisms and liturgy are full of truth and beauty. I think it's safe to say that I am more familiar with Orthodox spirituality and truth than most people in the Orthodox Church. These precious people have been a defense against radical Islam for centuries. They hid in forests and caves to worship Jesus when communism swept through Eastern Europe. Their value in Christian history is inapprehensible. To this day, I read many of the prayers of the Desert Fathers and others. I'd recommend you do the same. But I want to be clear about one thing: there is no replacing the preaching of the Gospel with clarity. There is no replacing yielding to the Holy Spirit in a service so that He can move and touch those who are suffering. There is no replacing personal reading of the Scriptures so that hearts and minds can be renewed daily in the Word of God.

To be real, my dad was a church attender who was full of himself, and he would be the first to tell you that today. He did many of the "right things" but for the wrong reasons. He experienced what we all did at the time—the power of religion without the presence of the Person. Dad fought us tooth and nail. He was not one to mince words or play games. As I said earlier, he is a tough man. I remember him questioning me if he saw me reading my Bible. I remember the anger he lived with in his heart and mind. Looking back, I believe he wanted what we had, but he was too hard-nosed to admit it. Ultimately, things came to a head, and Dad told Mom, "If you take my kids to the Orlando Christian Center one more time, we are done. I'm divorcing you. You are dishonoring our family." My mom responded in a way that only she could. She said, "In all these years, have you gone without a meal? Have your clothes ever not been perfectly washed and ironed? Have I not been by your side every step of the way? There's one thing I can't give up for you. It's Jesus. I found Him, and I am not leaving Him." Needless to say, Dad didn't know how to respond.

Dad went to visit our cousin Father Sam Kalamaras, who had been filled with the Holy Spirit himself. In those days, there was a large group of Orthodox people who were being touched by God, many through the service at the Orlando Christian Center with Pastor Benny. Father Sam was one of these men. In fact, he was the one who told me about the book *Good Morning, Holy Spirit*. I remember the day he visited us at one of my parents' retail shops to pray for us. We all stood in a circle and held hands. As I held his hand, I felt electricity surge through my hand and into my body. He then stopped praying for us and prayed for me. The next thing I knew, I was on the floor. Father Sam was and is incredibly anointed and saw mighty healings in his ministry. When Dad got to Father Sam, he said, "I can't take this anymore. I am leaving Evelyn [my mom]. She is off at these weird 'born again' services, and she is taking my kids there. In fact, she is there tonight. Father, I have had the divorce papers drawn up. I am leaving her!" Father Sam said, "Theo, slow down. Relax. Why don't you and I drive to the meeting and you can check it out for yourself?" Somehow my dad agreed! So, they took the two-hour drive to Orlando. What a drive that was. Full of awkward conversation and silence. As far as Dad knew, he was going to rescue his children from this cult meeting.

Finally, Dad and Father Sam arrived at the church. We were already sitting inside worshiping near the front of the sanctuary on the left side. I was so caught up in the heavenly worship that nothing in the world mattered to me except for Jesus. A family member informed me that my dad had just walked into the meeting. I remember the nervous feeling that went through me. *What would happen? How would Dad react to this setting that was so different than anything he had been exposed to?* Not to mention, he had reiterated many times that he did not approve of what was taking place in meetings like these. So, my dad and Father Sam stood with us and the rest of the family. There I was with my eyes closed, singing to Jesus. Well, I guess I was half singing to Jesus and half praying to Jesus that Dad would get completely undone by the Holy Spirit the same way I had months earlier. I remember wanting to peek at him out of the corner of my eye to see his facial expression, but I was too nervous to do so. I couldn't believe he was there. Little did I know that he had not come to enjoy the meeting. His intent was to divorce my mom for bringing us there but was merely doing Father Sam a favor by sitting through the service.

As the worship ended, Pastor Benny began ministering to the sick. Looking back, I can't think of two more opposite personality types at the time than Benny Hinn and Theo Koulianos Sr. Yes, they had very similar cultural upbringings, but in all other respects they were polar opposites. My dad was reverent and serious in church. Pastor Benny seemed like a little child and was about as predictable as the wind in those days. My dad was a sharp dresser, but conservative. Pastor Benny wore the loudest outfits we had ever seen in a church service. Not to mention his hair was a world of its own. Dad spoke calmly and directly. Benny, on the other hand, spoke so loudly that his voice echoed in your head for three hours after a meeting. Personally, I could have cared less about these things. All I knew was that Pastor Benny carried the Holy Spirit, and that was enough for me. But my dad's perspective was a different story. I remember thinking, "What is going through Dad's head right now? What does he think of all this?" Little did I know something amazing was happening in my dad's soul.

When the prayer time began, Pastor Benny began to call people forward who had been healed. Once they shared their testimony, he would pray for them. Many of these precious people would fall to the ground under the power of God. This was just too much for Dad. Let's be real here. He was in a church with no icons, no stained glass, no incense, no robed clergy, no chanting...nothing. The building looked like an auditorium, not a church. Now, add people falling on the ground, people speaking in tongues, music, and the offering to the equation. Dad thought he had gone to Mars. About this time, a young lady carrying a baby on her shoulder walked onto the platform for prayer. This was the moment Dad began to speak with God. In a nutshell, Dad said, "Okay God, I don't believe in all this falling stuff. These adults can fake it. This baby, however, cannot fake it. Here's my challenge"—can you picture the God of the universe laughing at my dad's challenge?—"let the adult feel nothing, and let the baby react to Benny's prayer." So, Pastor Benny approached the young lady and touched her. Nothing happened to her visibly. Then, he gently touched the little baby who was being held against the mother's shoulder. Instantly, the baby's head fell to the side and gently landed on the mother's shoulder. The baby was noticeably touched by the Holy Spirit!

Instantly, my dad felt what he described as a sledge hammer hit his chest, and he went flying backward through the air. He hit the pew and slid to the floor at the feet of his entire family! I could not believe my eyes. None of us could. There we were, looking down at this tough, cultured, military man on the floor and completely unable to control himself as he seemingly began to hyperventilate on the floor. Tears were running down his cheeks. My friend, God met Dad's challenge. Did He ever meet the challenge! I'm sure some of the family were in tears. Personally, I was in complete shock and thanksgiving. Dad had been touched by God, and God knew exactly how to humble my dad with His strength and love. After about thirty minutes, Dad stood up and gave his heart to Jesus. He got saved—I mean really saved. He became addicted to the Scriptures and to prayer. Before we knew it, he was the one driving us three hours each way to go to church. Today, Dad is a full-time pastor and Bible teacher who has seen miracles all over the world. One of the greatest miracles is that he travels with me and teaches in our conferences. Maybe you are believing for a family member to meet Jesus. Don't ever give up. Ask the Holy Spirit to touch that person just like He touched my dad. If He did it for my family, He will do it for yours.

Chapter Four

GRAND ENTRANCE

In 2006, as I was sleeping, the Lord took me into a vision in the night. I was standing on the eastern Mediterranean Sea. The air was crisp. There was a cool breeze blowing. The atmosphere was completely heavenly. Joy filled my soul. All of a sudden, a stairwell shot up violently from the Mediterranean, pierced the clouds, and went straight into the heavens. Someone I admire and love very much appeared in the dream. When this servant of God stood on the stairwell and began to walk upward, he said, "Follow me." As I followed him, I looked down and saw millions upon millions of eastern Mediterranean people following us up the stairwell. I'll never forget the beauty of the stairwell. It was a shade of white that I just cannot describe. Its purity was amazing. It seemed to be made of heavenly ivory or pearl. I saw Greeks, Turks, Lebanese, Israelis, Syrians, Cypriots, and many others finding this beautiful stairwell and following us up into the heavens. As we got into the clouds, the stairwell became much steeper. Instantly, it narrowed and the rails fell off. The wind picked up, and I remember thinking,

"Oh my gosh, I'm going to fall." The man in front of me turned back and said, "Just walk. Just walk." And as we continued to walk, multiplied millions followed us into Heaven.

When I woke up, I was shocked to my core. In the ministry world, that region is known as the "preacher's graveyard." I've heard many say that it's closed off, it's bound with religion, it's hardened. But I'm here to tell you that a great and historical outpouring of the Holy Spirit will break out in the eastern Mediterranean in the Middle East and millions of Orthodox Christians, Muslims, and Jews will walk into Heaven as they gaze upon Jesus.

I'll never forget the sense of urgency and hope that I felt after that encounter. As you know, I am a Greek, and to see God's plan for this region touched my heart deeply. It birthed a desire in my heart to preach the Gospel in Greece one day. So, I waited and waited year after year, asking the Lord, "When will I go to Greece?" A few years later, I tried to go. To be honest, I knew in my heart it wasn't God's timing, but my eagerness got in the way so I tried to push a door down. I can tell you now that never works. Finally, in 2012, this desire became a reality; doors began to open. I reached out to dear friends of mine, the Stimanti family, and told them what had happened to me in that encounter. They began to open doors around the country for me, and we planned a twenty-six-day trip from city to city throughout the nation of Greece and the nation of Cyprus.

At Jesus Image, we believe in fasting and prayer. Our desire is to know the Lord more, and if Jesus fasted, we fast. So, we called a forty-day fast, and we began to seek the Lord. We weren't seeking the Lord for the sake of going to Greece. We were just seeking the Lord to know Him more and to discover His love. One night toward the end of the fast, something happened that I'll never forget. I was sleeping and instantly I was in the Spirit. I was lying there in my bed, but I knew I had been taken into a new realm, a realm of the Spirit. My wife,

Jessica, was lying next to me. This is an experience that is difficult to explain with words alone. I can assure you it was more real than the book you're reading right now.

As I looked toward my bedroom door, I saw about six to eight evil spirits come into my room and begin to harass me and torment me. They began to curse and say vile things. They began to try to inflict fear in my life. I would say the name of Jesus, and they would withdraw, only to return again in just a few seconds. I tried everything. I quoted Scriptures. I claimed the blood. I rebuked them. While these efforts would get rid of the spirits for a moment, they would constantly return. This began to wear me down. I was extremely tired and, I must say, a bit fearful. After this went on for some time, I heard the Lord say, "You fought enough. Now simply lean on Me and worship Me." And so, that's what I did. Like a little child, I leaned into the beauty of the Lord. It was as if the side of my face was on His chest and I rested in Him. Oh, I felt the breakthrough—an incredible breakthrough. With my own ears, I heard a knock on the wall to the right of my bed. A ball of light pierced the room. Immediately, those spirits were gone. Needless to say, I was blown away. I could not believe what just happened to me. I then heard a voice. It was the voice of the Lord. He said to me, "Because you fasted and prayed, I have now given you the keys for breakthrough in Greece. I have given you this nation. You don't have to fast and pray when you get there now. The victory is already yours. Just go and preach the Gospel." So, that's what I did.

I landed in Athens and made my way to Thessaloniki. After a few meetings in Thessaloniki, I had a healing service scheduled at a church there. A few hundred people gathered, and we began to worship the Lord. The presence of God was beautiful. Once I felt the Lord's presence saturate the meeting, I began to preach. I've learned to do that. I've learned to wait until He's real to me to start preaching. You see, when He's real to us, we actually have something to talk about because we're leading people to a person that we're experiencing in the moment. But something happened in that meeting that we had never experienced before. After the preaching, we began to worship the Lord again. Many were saved, and it was a time of celebration. During the worship, a physical wind blew from the right side of the pulpit and began to fill the room. I will never forget what happened. People began to scream, they began to cry, they began to shout and laugh, and I knew that the Lord was healing people.

One girl had entered the service wearing a back brace, and when the Holy Spirit blew through that room, her back began to audibly pop. She physically felt her back realign, and her mother heard her back pop back in place. So, the girl tore her brace off and came to the platform to testify. I'll never forget that moment as long as I live. Two other girls were called forward to the platform. They were set free and filled with the Holy Spirit. It was like He came and worked so quickly that we could not keep up with what He was doing. You see, when He comes, you know it. I've heard some people say, "Well, I think the Holy Spirit's working in my life. I think He's working in my ministry." If there's one thing I can promise you, it's this: when He does, you know He's there. When He's working, you know He's working. When He touches your life, you'll never be the same. If He's really moving, if He's really come, there will be no doubt in your mind that He's there. Let's remember that He is God Almighty.

He loves to make a statement. Do you remember that when Solomon finished the temple, there were 120 priests sounding trumpets? Second Chronicles 5:13-14 says that *"...the house of the Lord...was filled with a cloud, so that the priests could not continue ministering because of the cloud; for the glory of the Lord filled the house of God."* I'm telling you, when He comes and fills a room, He makes our job much easier. I used to know (or thought I knew) so much. I used to know what songs to sing and when to sing them. I would pray for anything that moved. I tried this, and I tried that. Then the Holy Spirit told me, "If you'll just create the setting and the atmosphere where I am welcome, I'll come and do the work." And you know what? He has, and He has never quit doing the work.

It happened again in the upper room. Do you remember the 120 that were gathered in Acts 2?

When the Day of Pentecost had fully come, they were all with one accord in one place. And suddenly there came a sound from heaven, as of a rushing mighty wind, and it filled the whole house where they were sitting. Then there appeared to them divided tongues, as of fire, and one sat upon each of them. And they were all filled with the Holy Spirit and began to speak with other tongues, as the Spirit gave them utterance (Acts 2:1-4).

This was a fulfillment of the promise from Joel 2:28-29: *"...I will pour out My Spirit on all flesh; your sons and your daughters shall prophesy. Your old men shall dream dreams, your young men shall see visions. And also on My menservants and on My maidservants, I will pour out My Spirit in those days."* He is the King of a mighty entrance. Just think tongues of fire, a thunderous wind—this is a demonstration of power. He came to earth in an incredible manner.

I'll never forget hosting Steve Hill, the great evangelist from the Brownsville Revival, at our church in Southern California. Steve was a dear friend of mine with whom I became close. He traveled with our crusade team and with my father-in-law, Pastor Benny, for years, and was a dear friend of the family. When he preached for me at the church, I asked him, "Steve, tell me what happened when the Lord came that first Father's Day at Brownsville? What did it feel like? What was the moment like? I have to know."

He said, "I stood on the platform, and I heard a sound behind me. It sounded like a huge wave coming. People turned around to look, and there was no wave; but instantly I pulled up my pant legs because it felt like I was standing in water. I looked down, and there was no water. Then I realized the Holy Spirit's here and revival came."

Or how about John Wesley? When he would preach the Gospel, he would tell the people, "Come down out of the trees because when I preach, the Holy Spirit comes, and you'll fall out of the trees."

I'm often asked, "Why do people fall in your meetings?" My answer is simple: "Because God touches them." It's an easy equation: God versus the people. If He touches them, He wins. That's not to say that everybody who's been touched necessarily falls, but for those who do, that is the way that God manifests Himself in touching them. Why is it so difficult to believe that human beings cannot stand when God's holy power and presence manifests?

Chapter Five

HOLY SPIRIT'S FAVORITE SUBJECT

There is not enough room in the universe to list all that the Holy Spirit does. He is the power that keeps what we know as life intact. He is the air we breathe and the literal energy of the Godhead. I believe that we will have a glimpse into His amazing role and power when we are in Heaven. The appreciation for the Holy Spirit will continue to unfold in hearts for thousands upon thousands of years. On top of this, He is a real person with feelings and desires.

However, God's will is that we see His greatness while we are here on earth. As great and awesome as the Holy Spirit is, He does have a passion that is above any other. He may communicate on many levels and in different ways. He whispers to some and shakes others. To some He speaks through an ocean and to others through the beauty of a desert sunrise. Some enjoy a prayer closet while others see Him on every tree and in every breeze. One thing is certain, my friend: within the various methods, tones, and scenes through which the Holy Spirit speaks, He really only says one thing...JESUS.

The Holy Spirit is absolutely consumed with the beauty of Jesus. He thinks Jesus is just amazing. Now, this does not mean that He is less in nature or deity than Jesus. Absolutely not! Rather, the Holy Spirit's focus on Jesus lets us into the very heartbeat of the Holy Spirit and, for that matter, the nature of the entire Trinity. The Father, Son, and Holy Spirit are always pointing us to another member of the Godhead. This quality is so beautiful and highlights an aspect of God that I believe is far too often overlooked in the Church today— the humility of God. When is the last time you heard a teaching on humility in a Sunday morning church service, on television, or on social media? Humility is not just something humans (should) have. It is perfectly portrayed and seen in the character of God. It looks like this: the Holy Spirit points us to Jesus. Jesus points us to and perfectly represents the Father. The Father, in turn, says, "This is My beloved Son" (see Matt. 3:17; 17:5; Mark 9:7; Luke 9:35). The Holy Spirit is the One who makes it possible to hear the Father and see the Son. And the beautiful cycle continues forever and forever. Yes, my friend, the Trinity is beautifully captured by one another. As I say around the world to thousands and thousands of people, "The Trinity is not a board of directors in Heaven, trying their best to fix the world's problems. No! They love one another deeply and are in covenant with themselves. It is their deepest joy to reveal each member of the Trinity to us."

Now, let's get back to the Holy Spirit. It's so important for us to remember that there is only one member of the Trinity on earth. His name is the Holy Spirit. As I said earlier, He has one job: to reveal Jesus to us. Jesus said, *"He will testify of Me"* (John 15:26). That means the Holy Spirit wants to have a conversation with you and you can bet that it's going to be about Jesus! I'm often asked, "Michael, what's your fixation with Jesus all about? Don't you think you talk about Him too much? Maybe you should change the subject, man. There is more to the Christian life than Jesus." My response as to why I am so into Jesus is simple: it's because I've been touched by the Holy Spirit. You see, Jesus said, "...*out of the abundance of the heart the mouth speaks*" (Matt. 12:34). In a nutshell, that verse means that whatever is in your heart will eventually come out of your mouth. You will speak what's on the inside of you. Some talk about money non-stop, and others about politics, because politics and love of money flow through their hearts. Some talk about church all the time because the desire to have a big church fills the corridors of their hearts. Well, the Holy Spirit speaks of Jesus because Jesus is on His heart. And when the Holy Spirit comes to live in my heart and I yield to His passion and voice, His passion becomes my passion. His voice marries my voice. What He says, I say. Or should I say, Who He says is Who I say.

So, if you're wondering whether or not you have been rocked by the Holy Spirit, the barometer is very simple: Are you crazy about Jesus? I'll never forget the tender whisper of the Spirit in 2009 at our little apartment in Orlando, Florida. At the time, Jesus Image was a small, unknown ministry. I was preaching in home churches, storefront churches, Bible studies, prisons, women's meetings...you name it, and I was preaching there. To be honest, I still preach in small settings that most of the world has never heard of or acknowledges, and I love it. Back to the story. There I was, waiting on the Lord, and the Holy Spirit spoke these words to me: He said, "Michael, if the people in your meetings leave with a greater understanding of your ministry than they do of Jesus, it's proof that I have not led the meeting." WOW! What a statement. I began to connect with and understand the passion of the Holy Spirit and His feelings. He is passionate about Jesus. He is doing His job, which is to point our hearts to the beautiful face of the Son of God, gladly on the earth.

Why such a focus on the simplicity of Jesus Christ? Why doesn't the Holy Spirit just bypass Jesus and point us directly to the Father? Can't He just tell us about Himself the entire time? The answer is simple: a man can only know God through the God-Man. God's nature and ways are beyond our reach as humans unless we see Him in the Son. God basically said, "Look, I'm going to make this so simple for you now. I have been without form for thousands of years. My grace and love are causing Me to come to earth and wrap Myself in a body. I will literally be seen, heard, felt, touched, and followed. I am going to reveal myself to you as the perfect and visible will of God with a body. You will never ask this question again: 'What is God like?' Simply look at Jesus." My friend, never again do we have to wonder about the ways of God. If you are confused about God's perspective on sickness and healing, look at Jesus. If you are wondering about God's desire to provide for you, look at Jesus. Is God merciful? Look at Jesus. Is God bold? Look at Jesus. Should we pray? Look at Jesus. The point is simple: Jesus is perfect doctrine and our literal life source and model (see John 1). On top of these amazing truths, He holds all things together, and *"in Him all things consist"* (Col. 1:17). So, when the Holy Spirit points you to Jesus, He is pointing you to the Answer to your every need.

Beyond the Holy Spirit's motive to save you with a revelation of the One He loves, Jesus, it is also for the Father's sake that He does so. Perhaps you've never seen His ministry from this angle. Have you ever stopped to think about the incredible price that the Father paid as He offered up His only Son for a world that hated Him? Yes, Jesus paid the ultimate price, but so did the Father. He watched His Son get tortured and mocked. He offered Jesus to those that tied Him to a post and stripped Him naked before tearing His precious back open with the Roman whip, a whip covered in sharp bones for the tearing of flesh and lead balls for deep bruising. Imagine the heart of the Father as sinners assaulted His precious Son. A songwriter refers to Jesus as the

"Darling of Heaven." I love that because it paints a beautiful picture of Jesus' value from Heaven's perspective and, more importantly, from the Father's perspective. Not to mention that it was by the Father's design that His Son suffered. Jesus prayed, "If there is another way, let this cup pass from Me" (see Matt. 26:39). Clearly, if there was another way, the Father would have chosen it, but this was His perfect will—that Jesus die the death of the cross and be tortured brutally. Again, the Bible says, "It pleased the Lord to crush Him" (see Isa. 53:10).

This is a price that we cannot imagine. The Father offered His Son to the world willingly and watched Him get tortured so that you and I would belong to Him forever. I will never forget holding my son Theo up as I played with him. He was under one year old, and he used to love it when I held him up high. There we were, in my small apartment in Orange County, California. There was a small hallway outside the guest bedroom, and that is where I was playing with Theo. As I held him up high, I had an internal vision of the crucifixion. Holding my son over my head, I clearly heard the Lord say, "I gave My Son to be lifted up on the cross and to die. Could you give yours?" My spirit responded, "No! No way! I could never do that." The Lord said, "I gave My Son. I even gave Him for My enemies." Wow. The revelation of love that pierced me came wrapped in a picture of the price that the Father paid. I pray the Holy Spirit will open your eyes to see that the Father paid the ultimate price when Jesus died.

Well, what does that have to do with the work and heart of the Holy Spirit? What does the price the Father paid have to do with Holy Spirit's obsession with Jesus? It's quite simple: He is bringing the Father a reward for the price He paid when He sacrificed His beloved Son. The reward is a people who love His Son forever and who will be the eternal children of the Father. The Father sowed His Son, and the Holy Spirit is glorifying Jesus so that the Father will receive His harvest...you and me.

Chapter Six

HE'S ALWAYS BEEN THERE

The Holy Spirit is not new to the scene. In fact, He's been around since the very beginning of time. We know that He is completely God and has been in existence forever. He is not bound to time; time lives in Him. The Holy Spirit was the first to touch the earth. Before the Father and the Son ever graced the earth, the Holy Spirit was hovering over the face of the deep. We read about this in Genesis chapter 1. The Scripture says, *"The Spirit of God was hovering over the face of the waters. Then God said, 'Let there be light'; and there was light"* (Gen. 1:2-3). That's right, the Holy Spirit has been moving and touching and revealing God on the earth since day one. He still hovers today. In fact, before the Lord ever says a word, the Holy Spirit is on the scene, hovering and prepping the atmosphere for the speech of the Father to have its full effect.

The Hebrew word for *hover* carries the sense of an eagle hovering over its nest, protecting it while it waits for its eggs to hatch. This is what the Holy Spirit does today. He hovers over the water of our hearts. After all, the Scripture says that *"deep calleth unto deep...all Thy waves and Thy billows are gone over me"* (Ps. 42:7 KJV). Our hearts and our spirits are like deep wells of living water, and the Holy Spirit hovers over that deep. Before we're born again, our spirits are dead. Just as darkness covered the face of the deep on the earth in Genesis chapter 1, darkness covered our innermost being before we met Jesus. And so, the Holy Spirit begins to hover over our darkness, over our sin, over our blindness, and He slowly begins to touch us. He is the master at changing the atmosphere over our lives and our hearts. When He comes on the scene, He begins to moisten the soil of our lives. He starts to bring a tenderness to our hearts. This prepares our hearts for God to speak. When God speaks and our hearts are hardened and dry, it is difficult for His Word to take root and bear fruit in our lives.

I'm sure we all heard wonderful sermons before the Lord touched us. Perhaps we even heard the Gospel message preached clearly, but many of us continued in the life of sin even after hearing great preaching. What made the difference that moment we came to Jesus? What was it that finally caused the same message to stick and change us forever? It was the presence of the Holy Spirit. It was His loving hand breaking up our hardness, our stubbornness, and making our heart moist, giving the Gospel just enough room to take root in all of us. He is the master evangelist. The Bible says in Genesis chapter 2, verse 6: *"A mist went up from the earth and watered the whole face of the ground"* (Gen. 2:6). This is a beautiful picture of what took place in the Garden of Eden. That mist is a prophetic symbol of the presence of the Holy Spirit in our own lives. It is God's desire that our hearts become a Garden of Eden. It is God's desire that we never dwell in a dry land. The Scriptures tell us that the rebellious live in dry land (see Ps. 68:6).

The Holy Spirit is the Spirit of rain, the Spirit of moisture, the Spirit of fruit, the Spirit of color, and beauty, and growth. And this is what He brings our way. Once the atmosphere is prepped and He has done His work in us, He carries the power of the Gospel, which is the Word of God, into our lives. Just as light came upon the darkness in Genesis chapter 1, the light goes on in us. We can see. We're no longer blind. The face of Jesus rests before us. He becomes more real to us than anything or anyone. This is the beautiful work of the Holy Spirit. This chapter will show you that the Holy Spirit is not a new character who appeared in Acts chapter 2. No, He has been there since the very beginning.

THE AIR WE BREATHE

Genesis 2:7 says, *"And the Lord God formed man of the dust of the ground, and breathed into his nostrils the breath of life; and man became a living being."* God took mud and perfectly formed you and me. The Father is so meticulous. The Son is so precious and faithful. The Father willed our creation, and the Son administrated it. God perfectly put us together. The Bible says that He formed man of the dust of the ground by putting man in His own hand. Imagine the detail of the human body. Just think of the perfection that God has given us in our bodies. Our eyes, our veins, and our brain are more complex than any computer. Consider the way He's shaped us and designed us to keep disease away from us, the beauty around us that we're able to experience because of our five senses—all of this because the Lord formed us with beauty. The Bible says, *"I am fearfully and wonderfully made"* (Ps. 139:14).

However, even though God formed Adam with such incredible and perfect detail, Adam was still dead. His beauty did not guarantee him life. In fact, he lay absolutely lifeless while being perfectly and wonderfully made. It was not until God breathed the breath of His life, mouth, and heart into the nostrils of Adam did Adam come to life. Does this sound familiar to you? Does this sound like much of the

Church in the West? Beautifully designed buildings, chairs designed to keep you awake and keep you comfortable during a service. Did you know that church growth books and seminars actually tell you how to angle your chairs in a certain way to enhance the experience in the Sunday meeting? Did you know that churches actually determine the perfect temperature to keep the crowds awake during the meeting?

I've been in pre-service staff meetings in other churches where there is an actual flowchart detailing every minute so that the church-goer will be tended to perfectly. Now, I am not against excellence, or against technology, or against doing things the right way. If you're going to have a building, it should be great. If you're going to have chairs, why not make them comfortable? If you're going to have air conditioning, keep it nice in the room. These are all wonderful, and I believe the Kingdom is a kingdom of excellence. Let me go on. How about our technical packages? How about the screens, and the smoke, and the lights? Again, these are all wonderful, but we can all agree that there is an amazing attention to detail as it pertains to church life in the West. But I have question for you: Is beauty alone a sign that the church is alive? Do the multimillion-dollar buildings guarantee that the life of God is flowing through our churches? Do the cool outfits that our preachers, worship leaders, and bands wear tell us that God is on the move? Again, let me say, if you're going to dress, dress nice. I have no problem at all with being trendy and fashionable. I think it's wonderful. But I'm making a point, and the point is this: Structures, programs, money, construction, and crowds do not guarantee that God has breathed His Spirit into our lives.

If I were to paint a picture for you of what it looks like to be religious, it would be exactly what I am talking about right now: form with no power, structure with no cloud, speech with no breath. In fact, the Bible says in the last days that many would have a form of godliness but deny the power (see 2 Tim. 3:5). Let's look at our own lives. Is most of our time spent focusing on the details of what we construct on our own? Or is it spent obtaining and enjoying the breath of God?

FACE TO FACE

Have you ever wondered why the Lord breathed into Adam's nostrils? It's because to receive this breath, Adam had to be face to face with God. We must remember that at this point, Adam was dead. Adam could do nothing to receive the breath of God but lie there dead. This is a beautiful truth that I pray many, many more in our generation will understand—that as we lay there lifeless, losing our own will and dying to self, God begins the dance. It is God who draws near to us first, who breathes on us. What could Adam do before he was alive? Nothing but just lie there. Today, the very fact that you're reading this book is proof that God has descended into your life. Can you picture Adam lying there in the hand of the Lord after being formed and the Father so lovingly bending down and coming face to face with Adam? God literally touches Adam's face with His and breathes the Holy Spirit straight into his nostrils. This is what it means to come face to face with God.

Once Adam received that breath into his nostrils, he would breathe it out of his mouth. The first experience in Adam's life was to breathe out the breath of God, to release what he had received. This is true worship, my friend. This is true life in the Spirit. Once Adam's eyes opened, his first sight would be the face of Jesus Himself. Jesus is the face of the Father. Second Corinthians 4:6 says that *"The glory of God... is seen in the face of Jesus"* (2 Cor. 4:6 NLT). Only the Holy Spirit can open our eyes. Only the Holy Spirit can cause us to breathe. Only the Holy Spirit gives us the breath of worship. Only the Holy Spirit gives us vision to see the face of Jesus. I have been in meetings while ministering when the Holy Spirit's presence was so thick and tangible that I could literally breathe in His substance. With every inhalation I would receive His beauty and His glory, and with every exhalation I would release it in worship. He is the air we breathe. Now you know why Jesus breathed on His disciples when they were born again and said, *"Receive the Holy Spirit"* (John 20:22). Just think for a moment: This was the time when the disciples were born again, but had Jesus merely sat before them and never released His breath into them, the Holy Spirit would have never come to live on the inside of them and they never would have been born again. This tells us that the Son of God can sit right in front of you, but unless the Holy Spirit goes into you, you cannot be a child of God. I'm so glad that the Father, the Son, and the Holy Spirit work together so beautifully in our hearts.

Maybe as you're reading this right now, you feel the thick presence of the Holy Spirit. Maybe the room you're in is changing. Maybe the air feels a little different where you are. Perhaps an incredible peace is flooding your soul—all of your worries seem to be like faded memories that God is overshadowing as you read these words. That's because the Holy Spirit is right there with you. Yes, that's right. He's with you in that room you're in. In fact, He's the One that inspired you to read this book. This is His way of bending down to you, bringing His face to yours, wanting to breathe into you so that the lights would go on and you'd behold Jesus all over again. Just breathe in His presence. That's right. Stop what you're doing right now. Just take a moment. Give Him a few seconds and say, "Holy Spirit, I know You're here. I receive Your presence." Just breathe in His beautiful presence.

THE FAITHFUL DOVE

He also sent out from himself a dove, to see if the waters had receded from the face of the ground. But the dove found no resting place for the sole of her foot, and she returned into the ark to him, for the waters were on the face of the whole earth. So he put out his hand and took her, and drew her into the ark to himself. And he waited yet another seven days, and again he sent the dove out from the ark. Then the dove came to him in the evening, and behold, a freshly plucked olive leaf was in her mouth; and Noah knew that the waters had receded from the earth. So he waited yet another seven days and sent out the dove, which did not return again to him anymore (Genesis 8:8-12).

We all grew up hearing this story of Noah. I remember as a little boy being amazed at the number of animals, the size of the boat, and the incredible amount of rain and water that flooded the earth. As I began to read the Scriptures with a prayerful heart and more consistently, I discovered that as amazing as Noah's accomplishments in construction were, this story is not about a boat. As incredible as the amount of animals that found their way onto the boat is, this story is not about corralling a large number of animals. As incredible as the amount of water that covered the earth in that time is, this story is not about rain in the natural. Neither is the part about the dove flying away really about releasing a bird. That dove is the Holy Spirit. That ark is Jesus Himself. The window out of which the dove flew is the side of Jesus that was pierced on the cross. Those waters symbolize two things: the judgment of the world and the waters of baptism, both killing the old man.

Why did Noah wait seven days to send out the dove? Because it's on the eighth day that new life is promised. Seven means perfection, and eight signifies a new day. What was the job of the dove? The job of the dove was to let Noah know what the status was outside of the ark. And so the Holy Spirit roams the earth today, communing with the Father and the Son, sharing His feelings about what is happening in our world. Why an olive branch? It's because it's a picture of peace and a picture of the Anointed One who would be crushed in Gethsemane in a garden of olive trees—the One who would ultimately become our

Peace. No, my friend, the Holy Spirit is not new to the scene. He's always been there.

A Bride for Isaac

Let's have a look at the work of the Holy Spirit in the life of Abraham and Isaac. Genesis 24 says:

Now Abraham was old, well advanced in age; and the Lord had blessed Abraham in all things. So Abraham said to the oldest servant of his house, who ruled over all that he had, "Please, put your hand under my thigh, and I will make you swear by the Lord, the God of heaven and the God of the earth, that you will not take a wife for my son from the daughters of the Canaanites, among whom I dwell; but you shall go to my country and to my family, and take a wife for my son Isaac."

And the servant said to him, "Perhaps the woman will not be willing to follow me to this land. Must I take your son back to the land from which you came?"

But Abraham said to him, "Beware that you do not take my son back there. The Lord God of heaven, who took me from my father's house and from the land of my family, and who spoke to me and swore to me, saying, 'To your descendants I give this land,' He will send His angel before you, and you shall take a wife for my son from there. And if the woman is not willing to follow you, then you will be released from this oath; only do not take my son back there." So the servant put his hand under the thigh of Abraham his master, and swore to him concerning this matter (Genesis 24:1-9).

Remember, all of the Scriptures point to Jesus, according to John chapter 5 and Luke chapter 24 (see John 5:39; Luke 24:27). So let's have a look at the beautiful types and shadows of Jesus in Genesis chapter 24. Abraham is the Father. Isaac is the Son. The faithful and oldest servant of the house is the Holy Spirit. The father has a desire to find a bride for Isaac just as our Heavenly Father wants His Son, Jesus, to receive the reward of the Church, which is a wife and a bride. The servant, the Holy Spirit, is the One whose job on earth is to find a bride for Jesus. Notice verse 3 says, *"…you will not take a wife for my son from the daughters of the Canaanites, among whom I dwell"* (Gen. 24:3). In other words, the Father does not want, or will not allow, His Son to be married to those who follow the ways of the world. The Holy Spirit will not go— He will not offer union in marriage to Jesus for those who do not want Jesus. Can you picture the Holy Spirit moving throughout the Church as He prepares and looks for a bride for Jesus, the One He loves?

Finally, the servant found Rebekah in verse 15 while he was sitting on a well (see Gen. 24:15). Can you see it? The Holy Spirit and the Well. The Holy Spirit and the Well are always together. The Holy Spirit is always resting on the revelation of the Well of God, Jesus Himself. And so, the future bride, Rebekah, came to the well. Jesus only marries those who come to Him and want His water and the life that flows from Him. The Bible says, *"Now the young woman was very beautiful to behold, a virgin; no man had known her. And she went down to the well, filled her pitcher, and came up. And the servant ran to meet her and said, 'Please let me drink a little water from your pitcher'"* (Gen. 24:16-17). Did you know that the Holy Spirit sees you as being beautiful? And if you've given your heart to Jesus and live a life in His presence, you are a pure virgin in His sight. I love that the Scripture says: *"no man had known her"* (Gen. 24:16). This is a picture of being separate from the world, not tainted with the ways and concepts of the system of the world. Freedom from sin as a lifestyle.

Verse 17: *"And the servant ran to meet her and said, 'Please let me drink a little water from your pitcher'"* (Gen. 24:17). Oh, I love that the Holy

Spirit runs to us. As we come to the Well, Jesus, the Holy Spirit always rushes in. This is a place of incredible intimacy, as we see from the Holy Spirit asking for water. What does this mean? The Holy Spirit longs for the water that flows from our love. Our hearts are full of dripping water, and He is wanting to be loved and enjoyed.

The gifts of God—verse 22: *"So it was, when the camels had finished drinking, that the man took a golden nose ring weighing half a shekel, and two bracelets for her wrists weighing ten shekels of gold"* (Gen. 24:22). Gold speaks of divinity in the Scriptures, the nature of God. The nose ring symbolizes that the Bride belongs to Jesus. The bracelets on the wrist indicate that our work and our hands belong to Jesus. But these gifts also speak of the gifts of the Holy Spirit. It is the Holy Spirit who gives these gifts, just as the servant gave these gifts to Rebekah.

Verse 43 says, *"Behold, I stand by the well of water; and it shall come to pass when the virgin comes out to draw water, and I say to her, 'Please give me a little water from your pitcher to drink'"* (Gen. 24:43). Remember, the Holy Spirit is looking for virgins who love the Well, Jesus Himself.

Chapter Seven

RESTORING THE SIMPLICITY OF JESUS

I remember vividly the completion of a prior book I wrote called *The Jesus Book*. We were at a family dinner, and I was so excited to have finally finished a project that took me approximately eighteen months. As we were sitting at the table, one of my wife's uncles said to me, "Michael, I heard you wrote a book. What's it about?"

I looked up and simply said, "Jesus." I'll never forget his response because my heart broke for him.

He said in front of everyone, "Of course it's about Jesus, but what's it about?"

I looked back at him and said, "It's just about Jesus, period." I put my head down and continued to eat. I thought to myself, "How complicated some people have made the Christian life! Shouldn't the Christian life be about Christ? I mean, after all, if He does not come, what do we have? Shouldn't church be about the One who purchased the Church? Shouldn't reading our Bible be about the One whom the Bible is about and the One who wrote it? Shouldn't worship be about the One we're worshiping? And shouldn't prayer be about the One to whom we're talking?" It was at that moment I realized that simplicity needed to flood our hearts again.

Do you remember when you met the Lord? That moment when He became real to you? You didn't have theology or a Christian education, but you did have Jesus and you realized, "He's all I really need." You felt His presence, the presence of the Spirit, and instantly, His reality became everything to you.

For many, Christianity is about everything but the Person. It's about dos and don'ts. It's about weekly attendance in church. It's about a specific devotional time. It has become political to some and about social justice to others. While all of these are good and beneficial—in fact, I highly recommend them—without the person of the Lord, Christianity is dead. In fact, without Him, there is no Christianity. If Jesus is not actually in the room by the Holy Spirit when we gather, we are not having Christian meetings. You may as well join a country club or some secret society because it is His presence—and His presence alone—that makes anything we do "Christian." I've come to realize and believe wholeheartedly that the Christian life is the life of Jesus in us and through us by the Holy Spirit.

I felt like telling that family member, "No, you don't understand. You've forgotten the simplicity of the Lord. With all my being, my heart breaks because I want you to come back to Jesus and Jesus alone."

STRUGGLE

I remember when I was backslidden and away from the Lord, certain sins gripped me. I struggled in my mind. I struggled in my ways. I fought and fought to be holy. I remember walking into church feeling guilty and ashamed week after week. My parents pastored a church. My dad would ask me to get up and pray, and I felt like garbage because I was bound with sin. When a temptation would come, I would wrestle against it and rebuke it. I would bind and loose. Oh, I had mastered what I thought was spiritual warfare, only to find out that the temptation would grow stronger and stronger, even when I warred against it. This is when I realized that whether I was fighting it or submitting to it, giving the struggle attention was fueling it. So, to simply war against it was only making it stronger. Then I began to experience the presence of the Lord. This was the game changer. All of a sudden, He would come my way, and the Holy Spirit would brush my heart and pull on the strings of my desire. I would give Him my attention. I would talk to Him, speak to Him, and worship Him, and He would distract me with His beauty. His presence became so overwhelming that I forgot about my struggles. As we tend to the presence of the Lord, our struggles die on their own.

Ezekiel 36:26-27 says, *"I will give you a new heart and put a new spirit within you; I will take the heart of stone out of your flesh and give you a heart of flesh. I will put My Spirit within you and cause you to walk in My statutes, and you will keep My judgments and do them."*

How many of us fight to keep the laws of God but lose these wars day after day because we don't understand the ways of the Spirit? Following the Spirit, who is within us by default, causes us to walk in the laws of God. That is the beauty of the New Covenant. We call this the "law of life in the Spirit." As you yield to the Holy Spirit, you join the life of Jesus, and Jesus Himself has fulfilled the law. Maybe you ask, "Michael, how can I be free from sin?" It's very simple: give your heart and your attention to Jesus the next time the Holy Spirit asks you to. This is not an excuse to disobey the Scriptures; rather, it is the secret to obeying the Scriptures by simply looking to the Lord. So, what is the plan of God pertaining to your freedom? He will put His Spirit in us, and because His Spirit is in us, it will cause obedience to flow from within us, which is our deepest place, and this makes it simple to be an obedient child. There is a key to freedom that I would love to share with you, and it is this: True freedom is a Person, and your victory comes through His victory. When you fellowship with the person of the Lord, you connect with the victory of the Lord. His life becomes your life, and your life becomes His.

HE'S GREATER

It's so vital to know who we are in the Lord, but it is much more vital to know the Lord. Today, there is a great focus on the identity/ grace teaching. Let me say clearly that I love the grace of God. It's amazing and beyond comprehension. All we have is because of His grace. He found us. We did not find Him. Without His power and quickening we can do nothing. If you have accepted Jesus and are following Him, you are God's child. It is sealed! I believe it is so important to know who we are in the Lord, but it is far more important to know the Lord. You and I become who we are called to be by staring at Jesus, not at ourselves. Let me reiterate: We must know who we are in Jesus, but that only happens by knowing Jesus. Manifesting sonship comes by staring at the Son, not at us. So, to understand our identity is amazing and needed. This comes only by knowing our Father's face and voice.

The Bible teaches that we become what we worship. As the Scripture says, "They looked unto Him, and their faces were radiant" (see Ps. 34:5). That radiance speaks of the light and the fire of God. In other words, it's the face of God that our face becomes like as we look at Him. We must remember that while we are sons and daughters, we experience true sonship by being led of the Holy Spirit. The Scripture says, *As many as are led by the Spirit of God, these are sons of God*" (Rom. 8:14). To be led by the Spirit we must look to the Spirit because we can only be led by that which is in front of us. We can only follow that which we can see, feel, hear, and touch.

HE OPENS OUR EYES

Ezekiel 39:29 says, *"I will not hide my face from [Israel] anymore; for I shall have poured out My Spirit on the house of Israel."* When the Holy Spirit touches you, your eyes open. And what can you see? The face of God.

Do you remember what Paul said? *"Now the Lord is the Spirit; and where the Spirit of the Lord is, there is liberty. But we all, with unveiled face, beholding as in a mirror the glory of the Lord, are being transformed into the same image from glory to glory, just as by the Spirit of the Lord"* (2 Cor. 3:17-18). What do these verses mean? I've heard it said many times that they mean, "Well, the Spirit of the Lord is here. I'm free to do whatever I want." That's not what these verses are saying. God is telling us, number one, the Lord is that Spirit. That Spirit, the Holy Spirit, is not *any* spirit. He is the Lord. Number two: The Holy Spirit is not less than the Father and the Son. He is the Lord. Number three: There is a purpose of the presence of this Spirit—to bring liberty. Number four: The purpose of the liberty is to see the Lord as in a mirror. This is beautiful. This tells us that as we look at the Lord by the Spirit, His face permeates our face, changing our lives and our countenance into the face of Jesus.

Bob Gladstone from the Brownsville Revival said, "You cannot fake countenance." How true that is. I've met many people who are powerful and anointed servants of God. I've met people who have shaken nations for decades. I've met dozens and dozens of leaders whom God has used greatly, but there have been a few who have been a cut above the rest. There have been a few who have marked me. I must say, the ones who marked me did not mark me with photos of large crowds. The fact that they were famous did not change me. The ones who marked me were the ones who had something intangible about them. It was undeniable. Even with their flaws it was unmistakable. Their faces were different. Their eyes were different. It was as though at times you were looking into the face of the Lord. It seemed like their countenance, their disposition, literally became a container for the character of God. Some of these people you've never heard of, and possibly you never will, but one thing I can assure you: they will be champions in Heaven. Their reward will not be fame and television time. It will be proximity to the throne of the Father forever. It will be a crown of glorious presence that rests upon them in the ages to come. These people had eyes of fire. These people had joy and brokenness wrapped into their countenance. These people were as bold as a lion but supple as a lamb. They're hungry but content, needy but able to enjoy His presence. This cannot be faked. Whether on a platform or at home, the Lord seems to live in their face. Friend, this is true success. This is what the Holy Spirit does. This is what it means to become like the Lord.

Do you remember what the Scripture said about Stephen when he was martyred?

But he, being full of the Holy Spirit, gazed into heaven and saw the glory of God, and Jesus standing at the right hand of God, and said, "Look! I see the heavens opened and the Son of Man standing at the right hand of God!" Then they cried out with a loud voice, stopped their ears, and ran at him with one accord; and they cast him out of the city and stoned him. And the witnesses laid down their clothes at the feet of a young man named Saul. And they stoned Stephen as he was calling on God and saying, "Lord Jesus, receive my spirit." Then he knelt down and cried out with a loud voice, "Lord, do not charge them with this sin." And when he had said this, he fell asleep (Acts 7:55-60).

The Scripture says, *"He, being full of the Holy Spirit, gazed into heaven"* (Acts 7:55), and when he was done preaching and rebuking Israel, the Bible says that his face shone like an angel (see Acts 6:15). Do you know why? It's because he gazed into Heaven. One thing happens when you're full of the Spirit: Heaven becomes more real to you than anything around you. That's why just before he breathed his last, Stephen said, *"I see...the Son of Man standing at the right hand of God!"* (Acts 7:56). When the Holy Spirit overwhelms us and fills us, our first vision is of Jesus. Our heavenly home becomes our greatest reality until He changes our physical body. He'll even change our speech. Think of how Moses became after being with the Lord. Do you remember that his face began to shine? Why? Because his face took on the nature of that which he was looking at (see Exod. 34:35). Or how about the disciples? Uneducated men who preached boldly. What did the Pharisees say about them? "They knew they had been with Jesus" (see Acts 4:13). Why do you think the Pharisees knew they had been with Jesus? Was it merely because of the content of their speech? I'm sure that was part of it, but there was something more. Their words were spoken in a certain way. There was a certain tone to their words that was unmistakable. You see, when the Holy Spirit begins to change your life, He won't just tell you what to say; you'll begin to say things the way God says them. You'll begin to accentuate words in the way that the Lord would. So, God changes the filter and the topic. The filter is the heart. The topic is Jesus. When Jesus is preached with a purified heart, it just sounds different, and this is what the Pharisees noticed in those disciples. This is what the world is looking for: people whose faces begin to shine like Moses and Jesus on the Mount of Transfiguration, people who speak words in such a way that even those who are enemies of God say, "These men have been with Jesus."

To simplify things again, my friend, drown out all the noise. Eliminate everything from the Christian life that has nothing to do with

Jesus. Make it simple again. Begin to speak to the Holy Spirit, and ask Him to speak to you. If you don't hear anything, just wait a little longer. And if you still don't hear anything, then just wait another day. When you read your Bible, just talk to the Lord. Ask Him questions when you don't understand something. Before you go somewhere on a trip, ask the Holy Spirit, "Should I go?" The Scripture says, "If we draw near to Him, He draws near to us" (see James 4:8). Simple dialogue with the Lord is what He's looking for. After all, He is your Friend. Why don't you talk to Him today?

Chapter Eight

THE MORE OF GOD

D o you remember when Jesus said, "My words are spirit, and they are life" (see John 6:63)? There is an incredible truth hidden in this passage. When Jesus speaks, He actually speaks a language that is the Holy Spirit. So, picture it this way: When Jesus opens His mouth, the Holy Spirit is released as He speaks. When Jesus sent forth His word to heal that Centurion servant, the Holy Spirit began to move faster than the speed of light to bring immediate healing.

I'm often asked why I believe that it is God's will to heal. While I could debate it theologically, I've learned that doing so really doesn't take us very far. It is much better to demonstrate the power of God to heal than to argue with someone. But there is a portion of the Scriptures that reveals His will to heal very, very clearly. Do you remember when Jesus came into Peter's house and saw Peter's mother-in-law lying sick with a fever? The Bible says that *"He touched her hand, and the fever left her. And she arose and served them"* (Matt. 8:15). One of the greatest truths that illustrate Jesus' intense desire to heal us is the fact that He heals mothers-in-law! I love my mother-in-law, but I always say, "If Jesus will heal a mother-in-law, He will heal anyone."

Interestingly enough, He simply touched her hand, and the fever left her. Remember, Jesus told us to *"lay hands on the sick, and they will recover"* (Mark 16:18). Is there something special about our hands in the natural? These are the same hands that make breakfast. They're the same hands that pick up our children. They're the same hands that start our car. What is it about our hands or the hands of Jesus that are so vital? It's not the hands themselves. Those are merely the tools that God uses. No, it's the power that flows through them. And here, Jesus simply touches Peter's mother-in-law, and the woman is healed immediately.

If you would listen to the Holy Spirit right now, you would see that He is trying to show us something about the love of Jesus. He is trying to expand our revelation as it pertains to God's healing power. To Jesus, a fever is a big deal. To Jesus, even a fever must bow its knee to His power and authority. That tells me that God is interested in the most horrible sicknesses and also in a mere fever. The reason is that the same price was paid to heal a fever and to raise the dead. It was the life and blood of Jesus. So today, you may have a cold, or you may have cancer. Know this: Jesus wants to heal you now.

SIGNS AND WONDERS

Healings are signs and wonders, but there are certain miracles that take place that are not limited to physical healing alone. Jesus walked in this power during His earthly ministry. Therefore, so can you and I.

It's interesting that His first miracle was turning water into wine. Some people ask, "Why would He do that?" While I believe there are prophetic pictures and truths hidden in that passage that reveal the nature of God, we have to give God the right to do things simply because He wants to do them. I'm sure there were sick people at the wedding that day. Some might say, "Why would Jesus waste His time turning water into wine when there were people suffering?" The reason is…because He is Jesus and He can do things how He wants, when He wants, and for whom He wants. This is a beautiful example of the Lord performing signs and wonders to get our attention.

To be honest, I have seen many signs and wonders in my life that are outside the boundaries of physical healing. I have literally smelled the fragrance of the presence of Jesus in our meetings. Others have smelled a beautiful scent of frankincense similar to what is in the Orthodox and Catholic services. Some might say, "What's the point?" Well, the point is a deeper awareness of the presence of God. I believe that the more we give our attention to God, the more tangible His presence becomes. In fact, the Scripture teaches, *"As* [a man] *thinketh in his heart, so he is"* (Prov. 23:7 KJV). Our lives become what and whom we meditate on.

When Adam walked in the cool of the day in the Garden of Eden with the Lord, it was literal. That's right, he actually walked with God. He could see God; God could see him. He spoke to God; God spoke to him. He heard God, and God heard him. He felt God, and God felt him. This is a beautiful, holy life of intimacy that Adam walked in with Jesus. Today, you and I have been invited into this intimacy by the blood of Jesus.

Somewhere along the way, the Western Church began to view God as a concept instead of a person. I absolutely love reading the Scriptures. You will find a significant amount of Scripture in this book. I love my Bible. It is special to me. It has notes in it from people I love. I've wept while reading it, and I chew on the Word of God and feast on it every single day. But if we do not meet the Person to whom the Scriptures point, then they are nothing more than a book to us.

The Holy Spirit leads us to the Scriptures to reveal Jesus. He does not lead us to the Scriptures to reveal the Bible. My prayer is that God's presence would become more literal to you than you've ever dreamed or known could be possible. He is absolutely real—an actual person who longs to reveal Himself to us. He has a will, emotions, plans, and desires. There are things He loves, and things He hates. Some of what we do attracts Him. Some of what we do repels Him. He laughs. He cries. He judges. He forgives. He invites us into a literal, constant walk with Him. The more we walk with Him, the more our world becomes His. This is a very, very deep place in God. This is a place where He actually begins to break into our physical world and lives.

Do you remember when Jesus went up the mountain to pray during His transfiguration? The Bible says that He began to shine like the sun (see Matt. 17:2). His physical body began to take on the nature of who He was on the inside. This transfiguration was triggered by Jesus beholding His Father. Instantly, a cloud hovered over Him, and the voice of the Father came from the cloud. My friend, these are signs and wonders...all because Jesus decided to give His attention to His Father in Heaven.

Time and time again, the life of Jesus showed us signs and wonders. Today, the Holy Spirit is still passionate about pointing us to Jesus through signs and wonders.

A DEEPER BAPTISM

God has the ability to feed us and still keep us hungry. He has this way about Him that rewards us so that we will go after more. What I love about the Lord is that there is always more to discover in Him.

In 2003, I became the assistant to my father-in-law. These were incredible times of impartation and mentoring that I treasure dearly. I remember being in the crusades and seeing thousands of people healed miraculously. As I began to step out in faith, I began to see people healed when I prayed for them in those meetings.

In 2005, Jessica and I became the pastors of a local church in Orange County. When I began to pray for the sick in our church services, I rarely saw anyone healed, yet when I prayed for the sick in the crusades, many were healed. This was a very difficult season for me. The Lord showed me that as I came into agreement in the crusades for miracles, miracles were taking place under the umbrella of the anointing that God had given my father-in-law. However, in my meetings, there were very few healings. The school of the Holy Spirit is a thorough school. It is definitely a school of hard knocks and reality. I learned very quickly that if the people coming to our services were going to be set free, as Jesus promised, that I needed my own encounter with God.

I was baptized in the Spirit in 1989, but I personally believe that God has more than one power encounter for us, so that for every level in God that we pursue, an actual experience with Him is required to thrust us into that place. So, I began to fast and pray. I began to go after God. I began to seek Him for hours each day. Fasting became a normal part of my life. I started reading the books of those who had seen breakthrough and carried the power of the Holy Spirit to their generation. Kathryn Kuhlman became a hero to me. I studied her videos. I read her books. I began to visit Oral Roberts at his home as much as I could. I began to watch the videos of A. A. Allen, Jack Coe, and William Branham. I no longer sat through my father-in-law's meetings the same way. I began to study how he stewarded the anointing. I began to ask questions. I began to listen to the teachings of Bill Johnson. I began to study the history of the healing movement through the generations, regardless of their denominations. I was hungry for more in my life.

I came to the place where I told the Lord, "If You don't show in this ministry the way You did in the Scriptures, what's the point of me even being in the ministry? The world doesn't need another gifted speaker. The Church doesn't need more organized meetings. We ultimately need You, Lord. I need You, and if You don't come, I just don't want to do this anymore." So, weeks turned into months, months turned into long seasons, and I continued to pray for the sick and saw little breakthrough. But by the grace of God, I told myself and the Lord, "I will not quit until You touch me." As time passed, I had ups and downs. Some people I prayed for died, some were healed, but at that time there were no major healings.

A friend of mine named Bruce Hughes came to me and said, "Would you like to play a special golf course in the Northeast that has hosted the U.S. Open?"

I said, "I would love to play that golf course." I've watched on television many major championships that were held there.

So, he and his son Austin set up a golf trip, and we went. The member of the golf course who enabled us to play was a Lutheran pastor named Paul Teske. I had heard that he was a Charismatic pastor who prayed for the sick and had some type of a connection with my father-in-law and a few close friends of ours.

I remember that round of golf very vividly. Aside from it being an incredible course, it was the first time in a few years that I had walked eighteen holes. My feet were hurting, my back was tight, and it was a physical challenge. I remember Paul walking very quickly and not struggling at all. I also remember him taking some Advil, but nevertheless, he was still doing a great job. I can remember thinking, "How is it that this guy in his sixties is walking faster than me and doesn't seem to be tired at all?" It was at that point that he came up to me when I was walking down one of the fairways and said, "Hey, did you know I used to be crippled in one of my legs and God healed me?" I was blown away. When he said that, I instantly felt something deep in my belly begin to stir. I heard the voice of the Holy Spirit say, "Today is your day. What you've been praying for is going to happen. I am going to touch you." Faith erupted in me.

Paul then looked at me and said, "Why don't you come to our healing service tonight? I don't want you to preach. Just come and sit there and enjoy the meeting. You preach a lot; you could use a nice refreshing time." We rushed back to the hotel, washed up, and went straight to the service.

I felt destiny in the air. I felt that all the praying, all the fasting, all the studying, all the believing, all the hunger, and all the thirst was about to be filled by a faithful God. And as I walked into that church and crossed the threshold of the front door, Austin looked at me and said, "Hey dude, you ever feel like something's about to happen to you?"

It was the eeriest, weirdest question I'd ever been asked in a church. When he said it, I felt the presence of God. I looked back at him quickly and said, "Yeah, I do."

He replied, "Okay," and casually walked away like it was no big deal. I knew God was speaking.

As we entered the sanctuary, a young man who had done some work with Youth With A Mission (YWAM) grabbed his guitar. He was wearing sandals, jeans, and a T-shirt. He began to lead us in worship. To this day, I don't remember the song. I don't remember who was sitting in front of me or behind me. I only remember that Jesus walked into that room and it seemed that around Him was a tornado of the precious Holy Spirit.

As I closed my eyes, everything disappeared. My surroundings in the natural meant nothing. My challenges vanished. My worries were long gone, my aspirations dead. It was as though the power of God collided with my frail body. I felt a cool breeze go over me like a blanket. My heart began to race so quickly that you could see it beating out of my chest. My hands were bright red, and they were throbbing too. It actually felt like my heart had descended into my hands. I began to drip sweat. I began to cry. I felt like laughing but instead kept crying. I held on to the pew in front of me so that I could stay on my feet. I remember thinking, "Certainly everybody in this church must be feeling this amazing power."

As I opened my eyes to look around me, I noticed that everyone else seemed to be going through the motions like they would in any other Wednesday night service. It was then that I knew that God had reserved this moment for me, that I was on His mind, that I was His focus. This meant the world to me. The thought that God had stopped all that He was doing to come my way was breaking me up inside. I did not want this experience to end. At the same time, I felt like if I breathed the wrong way, I could die because of the holiness of God. I felt the fear of the Lord and the love of the Lord all at once. Had He touched me with any more power I don't know that I would have recovered or that I could have handled it. It was overwhelming, but I didn't want it to end.

I knew this was the deeper baptism that John G. Lake talked about. I knew this was what the Bible spoke of in the Book of Acts when it described the Church being filled and filled again to the degree that the place they prayed in was shaken (see Acts 4:31). This was after the day of Pentecost. God is not interested in just touching us once. God wants us to live in a constant baptism in the Holy Spirit.

That night, as my life was being rearranged with holy fire, I will never forget the presence of the Holy Spirit. I remember thinking, "You actually came. You are faithful. You said that if I sought You with all my heart that I could have You, and You came."

I prayed a prayer and said, "Lord, if this is what I've been praying for, have this Lutheran pastor whom I've never met before give me the meeting as a sign. Have him ask me to preach."

When I opened my eyes after praying that prayer, Paul was standing about a foot away from me. He looked me in the eye and said, "If you have something to say, go ahead and take the service."

I took the platform, but this was way different. I felt a substance around me, beneath me, above me. I felt like I was God's. That I belonged to Him. That now He would do the work if I simply obeyed. That He would do the speaking if I simply yielded. And when I began to preach, I felt a fiery wind go through me. I had no idea what I would say that night. There was no sermon prepared. There was no time to study. Just me and the Holy Spirit. My friend, I've learned that "me and the Holy Spirit" is all I really need.

As I opened my mouth, I began to preach a Person rather than a message. It was as if the person of Jesus had been tattooed eternally in my heart and He was the only sermon my heart would allow me to preach. As I preached Jesus that night by the Holy Spirit, it was as though bricks were falling on hard hearts. I could feel His convicting presence touching those who wanted nothing to do with Him. It was as if the whole room had been infused with new air. The atmosphere had changed. It was because He had come.

I remember calling forward the people who wanted Jesus, and it seemed like the whole church ran up to the front. I prayed for the sick and left the service. I will never forget lying in my bed that night at the hotel, still feeling electric currents going through my body. I wanted to tell someone about my new experience with the Holy Spirit. You see, it was more than a dream come true. God had come to me. He really came.

I called Jessica. I said, "Babe, I had an encounter with God tonight." Then I called my mom, and the moment she heard my voice, without me even saying I had an encounter, the tone of my voice alone caused her to weep in tears.

Lying there in my bed, minute after minute, hour after hour, glorious presence, ecstatic heavenly delight, was flooding my being.

TEACHER

As a boy, I served in the altar at the Greek Orthodox church. It was a big deal in our family and culture to be an altar boy. We had to prepare ourselves and eventually be ordained. While I don't worship that way anymore, I must admit there are some beautiful traditions that taught me so much. One thing that stood out to me was the huge Bible that lay on the altar of communion. It was massive, very heavy. The cover was made of silver and gold. There were precious jewels embedded in the cover. Also embedded in the cover were small paintings of the Lord. To this day I still have never seen a Bible like that one. As large and as beautiful as it was, it was always a bit intimidating to me.

On the one hand, the grandeur of that Bible drew me to it. On the other hand, the sheer mystery of it made me feel like it was too grand for me to understand in any way. Yet I could not dismiss the magnetic pull of the Scriptures. At the age of about ten years old, I remember lying in my bed and hearing a voice deep in my spirit say to me, "Get up and read the Bible that's on your mom and dad's dresser." In our home, the Bible was respected, but we never opened it unless we were imitating and pretending to be priests, chanting the Scriptures in Greek just to make each other laugh. But this night was different. There was a literal voice pulling me toward the Scriptures. So I woke my mom up in the middle of the night, and I said, "Hey, Mom, if God tells you to read the Bible and you don't do it, is it a sin?" Well, the question shook her to the core. I don't know if she thought I'd lost my mind or that God was actually speaking to me. Even though we did not know the Lord intimately at the time, there was still a reverence and respect for His name and His word. My mom's reply was typical of her passionate Greek personality. She said, "Well, get up and go read it."

So, I grabbed the Bible, went into my parents' bathroom of all places, shut the door, and began to read the Scriptures. But this time was different. This time the voice of God, the reality of God in the moment, and the Scriptures were colliding right in front of me and all around me. Today I know that voice as the one that you and I have been speaking about all this time in this book. It was the voice of the Holy Spirit.

Jesus promised us that after He departed and went back to Heaven we would not be alone, that He would not leave us as orphans. He promised to send another, and He said, speaking of the Holy Spirit, that this person would become our teacher. Jesus said He would remind us of everything that Jesus ever told us (see John 14:15-17,26).

I'm often complimented after I teach the Bible. People wonder, "How does Michael see what he sees in the Scriptures? How do these things come to light? I've never read the Scriptures that way before." Well, I've never been to a long-term Bible school, but I have had the best teacher in the universe: the Holy Spirit. When I read the Bible, I always pray this prayer, and I do it with my children in our devotionals too. I say:

Holy Spirit, be our teacher. Please show me Jesus as I read Your Word.

We have to remember the Scriptures tell us that all Scripture is inspired by God (see 2 Tim. 3:16). So, what better place or person to go to for a Bible study than the author of the Scriptures, the Holy Spirit? The Bible says in First Corinthians 2:12: *"Now we have received, not the spirit of the world, but the Spirit who is from God, that we might know the things that have been freely given to us by God."* The Bible is full of promises that have been freely given to us by our Heavenly Father, but entering into them requires the work of the Holy Spirit, for He teaches us the Bible so that we might know the things that have been freely given to us by God.

One of the greatest revelations that we can receive as the Holy Spirit teaches us is this beautiful truth: our God is not a distant God or a slave driver. He is our Heavenly Father. This means that His objective in our lives is not to give us a formula or to cause us to be consumed with right and wrong and good and bad alone. The Bible tells us, *"As many as are led by the Spirit of God, these are the sons of God. For you did not receive the spirit of bondage again to fear, but you received the Spirit of adoption by whom we cry out, 'Abba, Father'"* (Rom. 8:14-15).

The greatest way to become aware of the fatherly love that God has for all of us is to become a friend of the Holy Spirit. As He leads us, we receive the love of the Father.

Imagine Jesus saying, "Don't follow Me, because where I'm going, you can't go." He told them, "But the Holy Ghost, He will guide you. He will lead you" (see John 16:13). The Lord was preparing the disciples for the life that they would have to live once Jesus ascended into Heaven. Because He is so loving, He did not want them to be shocked about His departure. Now, I can hear you asking right now, "Wait, I have Jesus. He's in my heart. He's everywhere." That's true, but how is He in your heart and how does He make Himself available everywhere? By His Spirit. Back to the Scripture: "But the Holy Ghost, He will guide you" (see John 16:13). One of the ways the Holy Spirit teaches us is by guiding us.

My favorite pastime is fishing. Even though I played professional golf, if I had to choose between fishing and golf today, it would be fishing. My father owned boats so I grew up on the water. I was raised in a town that was on the beautiful Gulf of Mexico. Just about every day I was out on the water fishing. I even drove to other cities to fish, and slept in my car. I waded through swamps and lagoons, cut my feet on oysters, read fishing magazines—you name it and I did it to catch more fish.

One of the best things you can do as a fisherman to become familiar with uncharted waters is to be on the boat with a guide. The guide takes you to all of the good spots. His job is not to take you about the water aimlessly or drive you into a storm. The job of the guide is to show you those spots about which most people just don't know. His motives are good. He drives the boat, he knows the weather, he knows the tides, and most importantly, he knows how to find the fish. Reading the Scriptures with the Holy Spirit is just like this. He takes you out into the water of the Scriptures, the vast ocean of truth, and then based on what you need, He begins to guide you to the different verses that become alive to you. He begins to show you Jesus in a way that you have never seen Him before. He brings you into a peaceful place, just like the guide on a boat avoids the storm. He knows the weather of your heart, just like that guide knows the weather in the area. His presence comes in waves and flows, just like that guide knows the tides. The Holy Spirit is the greatest guide on earth and in Heaven.

So, once I opened that Bible as a little boy, a relationship with the Lord began. The Holy Spirit began to answer my questions, and He would one day bring me to a place where I would hear the Gospel for the first time. But I was getting to know Him better, and to this day, that voice remains. It has become clearer and is a greater part of my life than I could ever explain.

Maybe you are stressed; perhaps you're full of fear and anxiety? Maybe you don't sleep well anymore? Maybe your thoughts have gotten the best of you? Have you wondered if you'll ever just be the "old you" again? Wondered if you'll ever have your personality back? If you'll ever smile again, laugh with your friends, and see the good in life? Wondered if you'll ever be able to control your mind? The Bible says, *"He leads me beside still waters. He restores my soul"* (Ps. 23:2-3 ESV).

The beautiful thing about the Holy Spirit is that as He teaches and guides us, He actually heals us. He leads us to a certain place; it is the place of still waters, a place of peace, a place of tranquility. And once He leads us to these still waters, He restores our soul. Our emotions are healed. Our will is surrendered to Him. Our mind becomes the mind of Christ, all because the Holy Spirit now is driving the boat of our life. He does not desire to lead us into chaos but rather to still waters. Still waters are deep waters, and it's in those depths of peace where you will find your healing. While He is all powerful, we must remember that He is a gentle teacher and a gentle guide who will never force His will on us or drive us. Slave masters drive; the Holy Spirit guides.

Much of the brokenness, and the pain, and the scatteredness that we go through is often due to our desire to live our lives according to the ways of the world. But the Bible teaches in First Corinthians 2:13: *"These things we also speak, not in words which man's wisdom teaches but which the Holy Spirit teaches, comparing spiritual things with spiritual."* When the Holy Spirit comes into your life, you begin to live according to another world, another kingdom. We begin to follow another voice. Our thoughts become spiritual. The eyes of the heart begin to look above. As Paul said, "I press on toward the high call of God in Christ" (see Phil. 3:14). This all comes from allowing the Holy Spirit to teach us.

When He touched me as a boy, I began to know how great and powerful His teachings are, how beautiful His ways are when we embrace them. Remember, Jesus said He wouldn't just guide us, but He would guide us into all truth (see John 16:13). Fear has gripped millions of lives. It has shattered families, marriages, and children. If allowed to take root, fear can literally cripple us. Fear comes from believing a lie, and it increases as we meditate on that lie. The Holy Spirit promises to lead us into all truth—not merely to speak truth to us, but to lead us into truth. And as we experience that truth, rather than living in fear, we live full of faith; rather than living on the defensive, we become proactive; rather than hiding in the mountains, we take mountains for His Kingdom.

Yes, He's a faithful guide. There are so many examples of this in the Bible. Do you remember Peter on the rooftop of Simon the Tanner? The Scripture says, *"...the Spirit said to him, 'Behold, three men are seeking you. Arise therefore, go down and go with them, doubting nothing; for I have sent them'"* (Acts 10:19-20). Peter recognized the voice of the Holy Spirit and yielded to Him. Again we see this happening in the life of Paul through the Macedonian call. The Holy Spirit spoke to Paul in a dream. A man stood there begging him to come bring the Gospel. Paul obeyed, went to Macedonia, and preached the glorious Gospel. And today I have seen with my own eyes revival in Northern Greece through my wonderful friends, the Stimanti family, all because Paul listened to the voice of the Holy Spirit. How about Philip and the Ethiopian eunuch? There Philip goes to Gaza. He sees an Ethiopian reading the Book of Isaiah. He runs to the chariot to tell that man about the Gospel. Why did he run? The Holy Spirit urged him to run. He was guiding him. Philip was getting caught up in the Holy Spirit's desire to get the Gospel to that man. And after that man believed on Jesus, Philip baptized him, and that man took the Gospel to Ethiopia. And Ethiopia to this day is a Christian nation. I've been there with my wonderful friends Reinhard Bonnke and Daniel Kolenda. I've seen hundreds of thousands of Orthodox and Coptic Christians and Evangelicals burning to know God all because Philip listened to the Guide—the wonderful Guide—the Holy Spirit.

Perhaps you've said to yourself, "What do I have to offer? What can I bring the world? I'm just an average person. I don't have a great education. I barely know the Bible. I have no theological training. I'm incredibly normal." You are the exact type of person the Holy Spirit enjoys using. Once we are convinced of our inability, it is then that He steps in to give us power. The Scripture says it is *not by might nor by power, but by My Spirit,' says the Lord"* (Zech. 4:6). The Lord takes average people and quickens them, just like He empowered Philip, Peter, and Paul to shake regions of the earth. Through the life of Paul alone, Asia Minor and Europe were Christianized. Between these three men, many nations of the world followed and continued to follow Jesus because of one reason: They yielded to the guiding presence of the Holy Spirit. And you can do the same.

How do you begin? Begin talking to Him. Begin asking questions. Begin waiting upon and listening to Him. Give Him time to talk back to you. Become familiar with His slightest nudge, His slightest whisper, and His faithful presence. That's right, my friend, He will take your life and change the world with it.

Chapter Ten

SPIRIT OF PRAYER

W hen you talk about the Holy Spirit with people and all of the amazing things that He does every single day, you rarely hear people mention the Holy Spirit and His role in prayer. If you do and you are from Charismatic-Pentecostal circles, you may hear a little bit about the gift of tongues, but there is so much more that the beautiful person of the Holy Spirit does in us as it pertains to prayer. In order for us to understand His role in prayer, we have to determine what prayer is and what prayer is not. I grew up hearing that prayer is a humble request made known to God. I don't completely disagree with that, but it is only a partial truth. What is the core of prayer? What is prayer itself? Let's have a look at what the Bible has to say about prayer and the Holy Spirit. Remember, He is the Spirit of prayer.

Zechariah 12:10 says He is the *"Spirit of grace and prayer,"* or *"grace and supplication"* (Zech. 12:10 NLT, NIV). Another way to read that is He is the Spirit who empowers the Spirit of prayer, or He is the Spirit of empowering prayer. In Psalm 109:4, God gives us an amazing picture of what is available in the Holy Spirit. Listen to the words of David: "Though I love them, they stand accusing me like satan for what I've never done. I will pray until I become prayer itself." Can you sense the Lord changing your view of prayer? By the end of this chapter, I believe you will discover the beautiful truth of our absolute dependence on and need for the Holy Spirit and a life of prayer. Or as David puts it, we discover that prayer is not only something; at the core it is Someone. He says, "I have become prayer" (see Ps. 109:4). What does he mean by that? Let's continue.

Bishop Kallistos Ware of the Greek Orthodox Church has some amazing insight into this realm of the Holy Spirit. I honor him and his writings, as they have been a great blessing to me. I hope they will also bless you. He says, "'When you pray,' it has been wisely said by an Orthodox writer in Finland, 'you yourself must be silent.... You yourself must be silent; let the prayer speak.'"[1] He goes on to say that the one who learns to be still in the presence of the Lord begins to "[listen] to the voice of prayer in his own heart, and he understands that this voice is not his own but that of Another speaking within him."[2]

Do you remember the words of Jesus? In Luke 11:1, the disciples come to the Lord after they see the Lord praying, and they say, *"Lord, teach us to pray, just as John taught his disciples"* (NIV). This is a loaded passage. First of all, the disciples were inspired to pray because they saw Jesus praying. If you want to inspire others to pray, more than you telling them to pray, they really need to see you praying. A life of prayer in our own lives will inspire a life of prayer in the lives of others. Looking back on my life, those who have impacted me the most are those who have lived a life of prayer. Their experience of God was visible to me as I interacted with them, and it was clear that whatever was happening in their prayer room was changing their lives and making Jesus more real to them than anything else. This is exactly what happened with the disciples. They saw Jesus praying and saw the life He lived, and they understand that whatever was happening when He was alone with the Father was the source of His life. And so, they came to Him after He prayed, wanting to learn how to pray.

Notice they said, *"Lord, teach us to pray"* (Luke 11:1). They did not say, "Lord, teach us to heal. Teach us to cast out devils. Show us how to do that walking on water thing. Oh, by the way, Jesus, I don't have any wine. Is there a five-step process to turning water into wine? That would be awesome." I mean, could you imagine Peter saying, "How many steps are in the process of spitting on someone's tongue who can't speak? I need to make a PowerPoint presentation on spitting in people's mouths, Jesus. Can You help me with that?" They knew that it was not about how-to methods but about the Holy Spirit resting on Jesus and remaining. And after Jesus told them in John 5 that He did nothing that He did not see the Father do, and said nothing that He did not hear the Father say (see John 5:19), they began to understand that there was a deep, unbreakable eternal connection between Him and His Father. They wanted the same. They knew that was the epicenter of all they saw with their eyes. And so, they said, "Teach us to pray as John taught his disciples to pray" (see Luke 11:1). Discipleship 101 was in the lives of Jesus and John.

Again, as we read earlier, prayer is not so much something we do; rather, it is the activity and the person of the Spirit of prayer. What is more important in the area of discipleship than teaching people to connect the real them with the real God? I would venture to say that we waste our time teaching theology and life application and fail to teach people that they can experience the Living God twenty-four hours a day, seven days a week.

Jesus' response is beautiful and very telling. Notice there is no hesitation. Also, it's important to see that Jesus answers directly. That tells me that this is a question He wanted to answer. It was a question that He was waiting on them to ask because it was important to Him. There were other moments when He answered back, when He answered their questions with a question. It seemed like He often would speak in riddles and parables when the disciples came with a genuine question. Not this time. This time He was clear and direct. I believe this was something He longed for them to understand. Jesus answered by saying, *"When you pray, say…"* (Luke 11:2). Notice there's a comma between "pray" and "say." My friend, if you're going to spend any extended time alone with the Lord, you will discover that there is a huge difference between *praying* and *saying*, and this Scripture here shows that beautifully. It is very important that before we begin to say and request things in prayer, we allow prayer to begin. Once prayer begins, we can begin to "say" in faith. Benny Hinn once said, "If I have ten minutes to pray, I worship for nine." This is a beautiful, beautiful truth. Allow the activity of the Spirit to moisten the moment with the dew of faith so that the seeds we sow in our words can take root in fertile soil. I have learned this to be true as I pray for the sick. I like to wait a moment and allow the presence of God to become more real to me than the sickness. I have found that oftentimes faith is available in a very special way in such a time. Why is this? Because faith is not something; it is Someone. The Bible calls the Holy Spirit the Spirit of faith (see 2 Cor. 4:13). Well, the same is true with prayer. Prayer is not something; rather, it is Someone. It's the Holy Spirit.

I remember, as I was studying and thinking about prayer, I heard the Holy Spirit say, "Michael, what do you call somebody who gardens?" I said, "A gardener." He said, "What do you call somebody who runs?" I said, "A runner." He said, "What do you call somebody who walks?" I said, "A walker." He said, "What do you call somebody who prays?" I said, "A prayer." I was blown away by the wisdom of God. It was this revelation that began to change my life.

Before I go any further or give it all to you at once, let's continue. Kallistos Ware goes on to say that in prayer "it is the divine partner and not the human who takes the initiative and whose action is fundamental."[3] Saint Gregory of Sinai said regarding prayer, "Prayer is God, who works all things in all men."[4] Notice his statement here: "Prayer is God working." Now, I wouldn't go so far as to say that, but I understand what he's saying. True prayer, if it is truly the Holy Spirit, is to be joined and not worked up. It is not something that I initiate but something that I join. It's not something I do; it is something that I am swept into like a river. The Bible says that we are invited to *"drink from the river of* [the Lord's] *delights"* (Ps. 36:8 ESV). Once you begin to understand that prayer is the activity of the Spirit and not the activity of man, it can be joined with joy and ease. Listen to Paul's words: "It is not I but Christ in me" (see Gal. 2:20). He understood that the experience of God did not depend on him but rather on the internal presence of the Holy Spirit within him.

The words of John the Baptist do apply to the life of prayer: *"He must increase, but I must decrease"* (John 3:30). That is why I can be silent and still pray. In fact, I can be praying while I'm preaching. The greatest meetings I've ever had have been those meetings where two conversations are going on: one, with me and the Holy Spirit, and two, with me and the people. The experience that people have in the seats often depends on the experience I am having with the Lord. My goal is to let my words be His words and His words be my words. What I am really experiencing then is prayer. You don't ever have to stop praying. Paul said, *"Praying always...in the Spirit"* (Eph. 6:18 KJV). Is he speaking about the gift of tongues? Partially; there is much more to praying in the Spirit than speaking in tongues. Praying in the Spirit is to be overcome by, to be filled with, and to join the activity in the Spirit until your life becomes a prayer. Again, Paul said that you are living epistles (see 2 Cor. 3:2). What does he mean by that? He means that somebody who has been given over to God and possessed by the Holy Spirit literally becomes a living letter before men and before Heaven.

In other words, if people don't know what God is like and do not know the will of God, your life becomes a living letter that paints a beautiful picture of God before them and literally teaches them the will of God. You become a pen and a letter in the hands of the Holy Spirit Himself.

Kallistos Ware also said, "Prayer is to stop talking and to listen to the wordless voice of God within our heart; it is to cease doing things on our own, and to enter into the action of God."[5] I absolutely love that statement. There are many ways to pray, but I am dealing with the core of prayer here, the foundation—that prayer itself is the presence and activity of God in us until we are completely taken over by the activity of the Holy Spirit.

I hope you're discovering that prayer is impossible without the Holy Spirit. More importantly, I hope you're discovering that with the Holy Spirit, you enter the very action of God. What a privilege, what a joy, and what an opportunity.

The whole point of the Christian life is to love Jesus. It is to live on and off of the same presence that saved us. The same experience that brought us into the Kingdom is meant to be the food that keeps us alive while in the Kingdom. In other words, it was the experience of God, the coming of the Holy Spirit showing us Jesus, when we were born again that brought us salvation. Now we are to live in and from the same presence as we experience salvation. When we enter true prayer, it is a manifestation of our salvation, our union with God. After all, that's why Jesus died. We desperately need the Holy Spirit to teach us to pray. We need His direction. We need His voice. We need His expertise. Oftentimes our eyes are closed to what He sees, and He wants to open them. Job 37:19 says, *"Teach us what we shall say to Him; we cannot arrange our case because of darkness"* (NASB). In other words, I have nothing to say to God right now. I need the Holy Spirit. I cannot see what He wants me to pray into. Therefore, Job says, *"Teach us what we shall say to Him..."* (Job 37:19 NASB).

Romans 8:26 says, *"In the same way the Spirit also helps our weakness; for we do not know how to pray as we should, but the Spirit Himself intercedes for us with groanings too deep for words"* (NASB). This verse teaches us many amazing things regarding the Spirit of prayer. Number one: *"The Spirit...helps our weakness."* Many of us are often weak—physically, mentally, and spiritually. The Holy Spirit promises to come and help us in our weakness and make us strong. The Scripture says, *"Let the weak say, 'I am strong'"* (Joel 3:10). Number two: When we don't know how to pray, *"the Spirit Himself intercedes for us with groanings too deep for words"* (Rom. 8:26 NASB). When we don't know how to pray, He prays for us. Again, this is much deeper than praying in tongues. This is a depth of prayer that is too deep for words. It is when our flesh cries out, as David said, *"for the living God"* (Ps. 84:2). The Holy Spirit's desire to reunite with the Father and the Son in Heaven one day is manifesting through our being. Remember, the Bible says that the Father is jealous of the Spirit within us (see James 4:5). The Holy Spirit tells us that we are welcome to be with God as our Father. Galatians 4:6 says, *"And because you are sons, God has sent forth the Spirit of His Son into your hearts, crying out, 'Abba, Father!'"* Just think, the Holy Spirit Himself cries out for the Father as He lives in you. Romans 8:15 says, *"Ye have not received the spirit of bondage again to fear; but ye have received the Spirit of adoption, whereby we cry, Abba, Father"* (KJV). This is a beautiful truth: These two cries become one—our cry becomes His cry, and His cry becomes our cry. This is a manifestation of Paul's words: *"He who is joined to the Lord is one spirit with Him"* (1 Cor. 6:17). In a nutshell, prayer is the experience of the activity of the Holy Spirit, and the result is this merging of cries, whereby we experience being one with the Lord.

Maybe you say, "I'm too tired to pray." Not anymore. Now that you've read this chapter, you've found that the Spirit is the answer. He is prayer itself. Remember the words of Jesus when the disciples were sleeping in the Garden of Gethsemane? He said to them, *"The spirit indeed is willing, but the flesh is weak"* (Matt. 26:41; Mark 14:38). Maybe the reason you've become so tired is that you've been doing too much in prayer. You've been activating your flesh. You've been pacing, walking, stomping, shouting. That can be of God at times, but many times it's not. Sometimes the Lord just wants us to sit there, find what He's doing in the moment, and yield our body and our will to His plan. The Spirit is always willing. So, what is the key? Join the Spirit. Madame Guyon said, "Prayer has now become easy, sweet, and delightful."[6] All who desire to pray may pray without difficulty because we can be strengthened by the grace of the Holy Spirit. Again, Madam Guyon said, "God, is only to be found in our inner selves, which is the holy of holies where God dwells."[7]

My prayer for you is that this chapter will cause you to enjoy and yield to the master of prayer Himself, to prayer itself, the Holy Spirit. Instead of bringing a list of our plans to God, why don't we just have a seat in the morning with a cup of coffee and our Bibles, maybe some worship music, and say this: "Holy Spirit, You're the Spirit of prayer. Where do You want to go this morning? What do You want to do? I know You want to show me Jesus because You love Him more than I do. So, I'm here, Lord, to see Him. How do You want me to see Him? What side of Him do You want me to see? I trust You, Lord, with my problems. I trust You with my concerns. But right now, I come to You for You and You alone." When you begin to wait after such a prayer and wait until God touches you, you will be amazed by the life of experience and encounter that will be yours forever as you pray. Prayer will become a continual divine face-to-face love dance with Jesus Himself. You will have revelations, and dreams, and visions, and encounters that will blow you away as you simply give yourself to prayer as David did.

Notes

1. Kallistos Ware, "Prayer and Silence," *Orthodox Prayer*, http://www
   .orthodoxprayer.org/Articles_files/Ware-1%20Prayer%20and
   %20Silence.html.

2. Ibid.

3. Ibid.

4. Ibid.

5. Ibid.

6. "Prayer Quotes—Madame Guyon," *Prayer Coach*, last modified
   2 June 2012, http://prayer-coach.com/2012/06/02/prayer-quotes
   -madame-guyon/.

7. Ibid.

Chapter Eleven

COMFORTER

I used to believe that if I lived a life of prayer, fasting, devotion, and obedience to the Lord, I would not suffer and go through difficult trials in my life. I am sure God was probably laughing at my mind-set. Now I know that such a life is basically an invitation to testing and trials. In fact, the opposite is true: Living a life after Jesus is a guarantee that we will go through difficulty. The Lord told us that we are no greater than our Master and that if they hated Him, they will hate us (see John 15:20). I love Peter's perspective in First Peter chapter 1, verse 7. He says, *"The trial of your faith, being much more precious than of gold that perisheth, though it be tried with fire, might be found unto praise and honour and glory at the appearing of Jesus Christ."* Again, he says, in First Peter chapter 5, verse 10, *"But the God of all grace, who hath called us unto His eternal glory by Christ Jesus, after that ye have suffered a while, make you perfect, stablish, strengthen, settle you."*

I am not telling you that all suffering comes from God. I think part of the confusion is what we mean when we say "suffering." Let me very clear: Everything that comes our way in life is not from God. Sickness is not from God. Depression is not from God. Poverty is not from God. A broken heart is not from God. Rejection, shame, anger, hatred, betrayal are not from God. However, Jesus said that we would be persecuted for righteousness' sake. He also said that many people in our lives would reject us and come against us because of our walk with Him (see John 15:18). The Bible is very clear that if we walk with Jesus, we will go through trials. After all, nobody lived a more beautiful, loving, and peaceful life than Jesus did. And yet, He suffered more pain than anyone.

It's amazing to see how life can teach us what we never knew was even available. I've always been the type of person to be loyal, to want connection, and to be there for those I love. I was under the assumption that everybody thought the same and had the same heart for me. Like you and many others out there, I quickly learned that not everyone is walking with the Holy Spirit. Ulterior motives are involved—greed, self-promotion, and other things. Sadly, not all Christians spend time with Jesus so that He can soften their hearts daily and protect them from these motives and perspectives. When these things find root in those around us, whether they know it or not, their ways begin to contradict the work of the Holy Spirit in those that are walking with Him daily.

I have seen time and time again those who once loved the Lord, lived peaceful lives, wanted unity and so much more, slowly but surely live lives outside the presence of God. They begin to spend more time on themselves and the supposedly important work they are doing than alone in the secret place with the Lord. This begins to resurrect old ways, old perspectives, and the old hardness of heart, which gives way to motives that are not pure, and little by little these motives and ways supersede the ways of the Holy Spirit. On the other hand, when you're walking in the presence of God, you're not interested in promoting yourself because you are constantly feasting on the Lord. You have no need to be recognized by people because your main objective is to experience the Holy Spirit. His presence becomes your literal food. Think of this for a moment: In John chapter 4, Jesus goes to Samaria and sits at a well and meets a woman there. He ministers to her privately. All the while, the disciples cannot find Him. So, there Jesus is, ministering to the woman at the well, one on one, and the disciples cannot find Him. Perhaps they thought He'd be with the crowds, but He wasn't. He was alone with a person who needed help. When they find Him— it's funny—they run up to Him and said, *"Rabbi, eat"* (John 4:31). Then He says to them, *"I have food to eat of which you do not know"* (John 4:32). What did Jesus mean by this? What was He saying? He explains it in verse 34: the Lord said, *"My food is to do the will of Him who sent Me to accomplish His work"* (John 4:34 ESV).

Jesus lived before the Father, whether He was on the shores of Galilee with tens of thousands in front of Him for a great miracle service, sitting at the well with one woman, or on the mountain completely by Himself praying. He did not live before man. He lived before God. Because of that, He ate the food of the will of God, which is the presence of God. Therefore, He was completely fulfilled. He never had to manipulate, promote, or wiggle Himself into some situation so that people would know Him better. He simply enjoyed the presence of the Father and obeyed the voice of the Father. The result of this was a life that shook the world in three years. These are the ways of the Holy Spirit, and when you live this way, what contradicts that will often target these ways. This oftentimes gives way to persecution. I have seen it in ministries. I have seen it in churches and friendships. When these two internal cultures collide, there can often be friction.

I have had to make some tough choices in my life that have led to ridicule and isolation. Time and time again, I have chosen the presence of God over money and notoriety. I have chosen the smile of Jesus over the applause of man. This has often caused conflict and persecution. My heart has been so broken that there have been mornings when I have wondered if I could get through the day. I have felt the pain of rejection. I know what it is to be maligned behind my back to leaders I respect, all because I refuse to compromise. This is the type of suffering and persecution that Jesus promised us. To be real, this is very minor in comparison to what millions of Christians face around the world. They know true suffering. They know true pain. As real as ours is, it's important that we remember that much of the Christian population is not even allowed to gather in public due to fear of being killed or losing family members. Our brothers and sisters in the Middle East are a perfect example of this.

I remember a story that touched my heart. My father-in-law was telling Rex Humbard about all the persecution he was going through. Rex, being the gentle, loving father that he was, just sat there and listened. When my father-in-law was done, Rex looked at him and said, "Benny, look down at your hands." And so, he did. Rex went on to say, "Do you see any holes in them?" and gently smiled. What was the point? As painful as our persecution can be, as painful as our suffering can be, take comfort in the fact that One suffered a much greater trial and endured much more brutal pain than we ever did, and His name is Jesus. It's in these moments, however, that we need a Comforter. We all need to feel the peace of God and the embrace of God in moments when people or situations bring trial, confusion, and pain.

I like to compare it to being hurt physically and showing up to a good hospital. Picture the wound in your body as the wound in your heart or your mind. The nurses are like the angels. They're rushing around to protect you, to make sure your vitals are functioning properly, to make sure that nobody's in the room who's not supposed to be there. And then eventually in walks this doctor in a white jacket with a smile on his face. He comes and puts his hand on your shoulder. Before he says anything, his reassuring smile brings peace to your soul. The hospital is much like the Kingdom of God. The suffering and hurting people of the world run in, and they are tended to, to be healed and to get up again. Jesus is the One that, no matter what we face, He's always there to bring us peace.

Second Corinthians chapter 1, verses 3 and 4, say, *"Blessed be the God and Father of our Lord Jesus Christ, the Father of mercies and God of all comfort, who comforts us in all our affliction so that we will be able to comfort those who are in any affliction with the comfort with which we ourselves are comforted by God"* (2 Cor. 1:3-4 NASB). God is a God of comfort. In fact, one of the names for the Holy Spirit is Comforter. John 14:26 says, *"But the Comforter, which is the Holy Ghost, whom the Father will send in My name, He shall teach you all things, and bring all things to your remembrance, whatsoever I have said unto you"* (KJV). Now maybe you're saying, "I need comfort, not remembrance. I need peace, not a reminder." Remember, the words of Jesus carry life in them.

Sometimes our suffering is due to a lack of vision and proper perspective. How we see things frames our world. The Bible says, *"As* [a man] *thinketh in his heart, so he is"* (Prov. 23:7 KJV). There are many times when I have suffered greatly and the slightest adjustment in my perspective literally eliminated the pain in my heart. The moment I saw things from God's perspective instead of the world's, or even instead of mine, things changed. One of the ways the Holy Spirit comforts us is by bringing to remembrance what Jesus said.

Another way the Holy Spirit brings comfort is by His presence alone. I can't tell you how many times I have been stressed and afraid, and I'll hear this small voice in my heart say, "Stop what you're doing and worship Me. Just give Me a moment to touch you." I personally believe that the Holy Spirit is just a whisper away, and His presence comes and settles our chaos. He wraps Himself around us like this blanket of peace, and without hearing any audible voice, there's a deep knowledge that everything is going to be okay. Acts 9:31 says, *"So the church throughout all Judea and Galilee and Samaria enjoyed peace, being built up; and going on in the fear of the Lord and in the comfort of the Holy Spirit..."* (NASB). There's something about the comfort of the Holy Spirit that changes everything.

Have you ever been so busy and scattered in your mind that things just seem to get out of control? Are there people in your life whom you can't seem to corral? Are there areas of life that have gotten away from you and that are moving at such a fast speed that you can't get your arms around them? And you're trying and trying to keep up with the demands of life, but the faster you run, the more the demands outpace you. And you throw your hands up in the air and say, "I don't know what to do anymore. I can't do this." And instead of you reigning in life as the Bible says (see Rom. 5:17), life begins to reign over you. Yet amid all of that noise and movement, deep within you there seems to be this voice, and the voice says, "Stop what you're doing, and just give Me a second. Stop what you're doing, and say My name. Stop what you're doing, and worship Me." That's the voice of the Holy Spirit. He's not trying to get you to stop what you're doing for the mere purpose of stopping, but He understands that in that pause, a doorway is created for Him to step into your situation, first and foremost to comfort you. Why is that the case? It is because you are more important to Him than your situation. We don't want to believe that, because we have a tendency to elevate our situations and responsibilities above ourselves and people. Yet the Lord is more focused on His inheritance, on the ones He died for, and that's you. He died for you before He died for an event. He died for you before He died for a church program. He wants you to be okay. And as you stop, He moves. Where does He move? Toward you. And the minute He comes your way and puts His hand on you like that doctor puts his hand on that sick patient, He brings you peace. Once He brings you peace, He begins to move into that situation and changes it, and shifts it, and fixes it, and takes care of it. The problem is we oftentimes forget to give Him the green light. His green light comes from our red light. What do I mean by that? The moment we stop for Him, He moves for us.

I am telling you there is a place in the Lord where, regardless of what goes on around you, you can live in perfect peace. Jesus promised us a peace that surpasses all understanding (see Phil. 4:7). When the storm was raging on the sea of Galilee, Jesus was sleeping on the bow of the boat. When the disciples were in chaos, scattered, throwing water overboard, He was taking a nice nap. I really love the way Bill Johnson describes this scene. He says that Jesus could sleep because He was at peace on the inside and He could calm the storm because there was no storm in Him. The peace in Him gave Him the authority to calm the storm around Him.

My friend, I'm sure there are storms waging around you right now. I'm not discounting that or diminishing your pain, but I can tell you there is a Doctor in the hospital of the Kingdom of God. There are still angels, like there are nurses, moving around at rapid speed, ready to help you, and realign everything, and protect you. I have yet to see anyone running on a hospital bed. Instead, patients are forced to take a moment to stop everything, to simply lie there. Would you do that right now? Would you consider just lying there in the Kingdom of God, which is His presence? Do it just long enough for the Doctor, the Comforter, the Holy Spirit Himself to come right now and put His hand on you so that you can see the smile of Jesus, so that He can tend to your pain, and calm you, and look at you like a good doctor looks at his patient and says, "Everything is going to be okay."

Let's just pray right now.

Heavenly Father, I'm stopping for a moment because I'm in pain and the world around me is moving so fast. I often feel stress. Walk in, Lord, and touch me. Holy Spirit, comfort me. Show me the smile of Jesus. As You touch me, I know everything will be okay. Thank You for being my comforter. Thank you for being my blanket of peace. In Jesus' name, amen.

Chapter Twelve

SEVENFOLD SPIRIT

Like the Father and the Son, the Holy Spirit has many names and characteristics. After all, He is a person. If there were one truth that I pray you would grasp as you read this book, it would be this: The Holy Spirit is a person who can be known. If He is a person, that means He has a personality. He enjoys some things, and others He does not. There are certain people that He is closer to than others. It might make us a bit uncomfortable, but the reality is that God has favorites. If it were not so, He would not have favor. His favorites are covered with favor. Of course He feels closer to some people than others. It's because He can trust them—and not just trust them with what He does; He can trust them with His feelings.

One of the ways He begins a relationship is by sharing His character with us. It's sort of like an introduction. He begins to show us what He's like and who He is. It's no different than you meeting somebody and saying, "Hello" and giving that person your name. Once you've sat down and taken some time with that person, you would begin to talk to him or her about who you are, your history, what you like, and what you don't like. He or she would then discover your character and your personality if you continue the relationship. This is no different than meeting the Holy Spirit, except He's more wonderful than anybody else you've ever met in your life. In Isaiah 11:2, He begins to share with us seven beautiful characteristics of His person. We call this the "seven-fold Spirit of God." Now, there are many other angles by which we see the Holy Spirit. He has many more names, but these seven are a beautiful place to begin exploring the depths of the Holy Spirit's character.

Isaiah 11:2 says, *"And the spirit of the Lord shall rest on him, the spirit of wisdom and understanding, the spirit of counsel and might, the spirit of knowledge and of the fear of the Lord"* (KJV). The sevenfold Spirit here is: 1) the Spirit of the Lord, 2) the Spirit of wisdom, 3) the Spirit of understanding, 4) the Spirit of counsel, 5) the Spirit of might, 6) the Spirit of knowledge, and 7) the Spirit of the fear of the Lord.

THE SPIRIT OF THE LORD

Let's begin with the Spirit of the Lord. It is vital that we understand that the Holy Spirit is the Spirit of the Lord. He is not beneath the Father or the Son. While He is His own person, He is still completely one with Them. Three in One—this is the mystery and beauty of the Trinity. The Spirit of Jesus is the Holy Spirit. The Spirit of the Father is the Holy Spirit. The Holy Spirit is the Spirit of Jesus, and the Holy Spirit is the Spirit of the Father. The Holy Spirit is the Spirit of the Lord. The Bible says, *"Now the Lord is that Spirit..."* (2 Cor. 3:17 KJV). While He is our friend, we have to remember that He is our Lord. He must be in charge of our lives. He is to lead the dance. Of course, He is the most loving person on planet Earth today. Yes, He is the most intimate being you will ever meet. He loves it when we cooperate with Him. He wants us to co-labor with Him. He loves to have conversations with us. He's a beautiful friend; there is no doubt about it. However, we need to remember that He is God Almighty, the Creator of Heaven and earth. Even the apostles knew this, as evidenced by the Apostles' Creed. The Creed has become a foundational statement for the Church world-wide. Listen to what the apostles said regarding the Holy Spirit in the early Church: "We believe in the Holy Spirit, the Lord, the Giver of life, who proceeds from the Father and the Son, who with the Father and the Son is worshiped and glorified, who has spoken through the prophets."

Since the Church began, the Holy Spirit has been known as the Spirit of the Lord. The Greek word for "Lord" is the word *kyrios*. It means "one who completely owns something." So, to say that the Holy Spirit is Lord of my life is to say that He completely owns every ounce of my being. It means that He has the right to tell me what to do and what not to do. He can tell me not to go somewhere. He can tell me whom to marry. He's allowed to say "no" to me. In other words, my life is not my own if the Holy Spirit is to be my Lord.

Years ago, I had a secretary who was a wonderful strength to our ministry. One day, she called and said, "I'm so sorry, Michael, but my husband and I have decided to leave the church and go begin a church of our own." I instantly knew that this was not the will of God, but I could sense in the tone of her voice—and being familiar with the situation, I knew—that her mind would not be changed. I knew her husband felt the same way. They were set on leaving our church and starting a church of their own. So, they moved across the country and started a church. We sent them off with love and a financial blessing, but something in me knew that I could not endorse it through the lay-ing on of hands and a spoken commission because I knew deep in my spirit it was not the will of God. My conscience would not allow me to do so. I often thought about them when they left, stayed in touch with them, tried to encourage them. I wanted them to know that regardless of my perspective, love would always rule in our hearts toward them.

After a few months, I went into a dream. In the dream, I saw them in their apartment across the country with the lights turned off, and I heard them saying they did not have enough money to pay their utility bills. I actually saw them going through their checkbook trying to find the money to pay for basic necessities. I jumped out of bed so excited that God had spoken to me. I was so thrilled just to hear His voice. These were days of deep prayer and fasting. They were exciting days and discouraging days. This was the season that I was so hungry for God that the lack of immediate breakthrough would cause discouragement in my life. So, just to hear His voice in a dream meant the world to me.

I got out of bed and called them. They did not answer the phone so I left a message. I said, "This is Michael. I just had a dream that you guys are unable to pay your utilities. I'm going to send you a check to help you out." I was still amazed that God would speak to me with such detail. I was on cloud nine. They called back immediately and said, "We're so sorry that we could not get to you on the phone. We were on the other line with the utility company because they turned our lights off. We didn't have the money to pay our electric bill." How incredible is God! They were amazed too. They said, "We can't believe that God would speak to you all the way in California and wake you up just to tell you that we have a need."

That day I shared the testimony with those close to me. I was still completely blown away that God took time to talk to me. A few days went by, and I began to speak to the Holy Spirit. I said, "Lord, thank You so much for talking to me about these people. Thank You for Your voice, Lord." Immediately, He said, "Michael, I'm glad you're thankful, but you forgot to write the check. I didn't talk to you just to talk to you. I spoke to you so that you would help them!" How the Lord puts up with us! He must have a sense of humor. Can you imagine—I was so excited to hear His voice that I forgot to send the check! This is a beautiful picture of how the Holy Spirit is not just our friend and lover;

He is the Lord Himself, who wants to give us direction and waits for us to obey.

One day I was sitting with Reinhard Bonnke over lunch, and he began to tell me the story of how the Lord blessed his ministry with a rent-free office building in Orlando. It housed the headquarters of Christ for all Nations and saved them tens of thousands of dollars per month. The story I'm about to share with you has been shared by Reinhard around the world. One day the Lord spoke to Reinhard and said, "Reinhard, I am going to give you a harvest home." He said, "Lord, what does that mean—a harvest home?" Instantly, the Lord put on his heart, "I will give you a building, a headquarters, so that you can house the needs of the ministry, the staff, and raise up evangelists to go around the world." Immediately, Reinhard got on the phone and called my dear friend Daniel Kolenda. He said, "Daniel, I want you to get ready. I am driving in to go look at buildings. Find me a realtor." Being a Saturday morning, it was very difficult to find a realtor, not to mention that the Christ for all Nations staff was off for the weekend. They drove around and did not find a building. Many people would think that it was a failed day, that Reinhard might have been better off just enjoying his Saturday doing something a little more relaxing, but he had a different perspective. He said, "I drove in on a minute's notice knowing I wouldn't find a place today, but I wanted God to see that when the Holy Spirit speaks to me, I obey, and that I jump at His voice." Hearing that story changed my life. Reinhard looked me in the eye, and he said, "God does not just wait for us to obey, but He watches to see how quickly we obey. And I want God to know that when He speaks to me, I jump with obedience." This is somebody who knows the Holy Spirit is not only his friend, but the Lord Himself.

In the early days of Jesus Image, I was invited to preach at a conference in Bradenton, Florida. There were about 250 people there in the crowd. The last night, I taught on the need to know and be empowered by the Holy Spirit. The room was filled with electricity. I can remember it like it was yesterday. It seemed like every word was a holy break that crushed the hearts of the people in a beautiful way. They were sitting on the edge of their seats, yearning deep in their soul to encounter the literal presence of God. To be honest, all I really do in a meeting is surrender enough for God to touch His people, and this night was no different. They wanted God so badly you could smell it. So, the moment came, after teaching on the need for the power of the Holy Spirit for about an hour, that I called them forward. They rushed the platform. It was jam-packed with hungry hearts. The worship began, and I could feel the presence of God come upon me like electric power. I stepped off the platform to lay hands on the people in faith, that they would receive power from on high. I laid my hands on the first person—nothing happened. Second person—nothing happened. Third person—nothing happened. All of a sudden, I heard the voice of the Holy Spirit instruct me and challenge me in the most childlike manner. This is what He said: "Michael, you're laying hands on them with the wrong hand tonight. Switch hands." Well, I had been laying hands on them with my right hand because I'm right-handed. Was I hearing God properly? Could the God of the universe really care about which hand I was using to touch the people? We're talking about the God who created the atom. The Holy Spirit is the Creator, the Lord Himself. He is the Spirit that hovered over the face of the deep in Genesis 1 (see Gen. 1:2). He is the breath of God. And now He was telling me that I was praying with the wrong hand. It didn't make sense to my sophisticated mind. I mean, after all, with all the verses in the Word of God and all of the in-depth study that I had done—all of the great theologians, the amazing sermons, the perfect hermeneutics, and the incredible orators I had studied—could God really speak to me about switching hands when I laid hands on people? It didn't make sense to the natural mind, but to Him it made all the sense in the world.

Without telling people, I tried God's voice out, and I said, "Okay, Lord, I'll switch hands." And the moment I switched hands it was like a bomb went off. Prior to the switching of hands, it was like a cemetery. After, it was like God Himself took the meeting. There were people on the floor crying, shaking, being filled with the Holy Spirit, speaking in tongues. I was blown away. I didn't tell anybody what was happening with me because I didn't quite understand it myself. I thought God was way too busy and far too deep to use a hand switch as a vehicle to touch people.

After the meeting, my wife came up to me, and she said, "Hey, I want to speak to you. There's something I need to talk to you about." She said, "While you were laying hands on people, the Lord spoke to me, and He said, 'Michael is praying for the people with the wrong hand. He needs to switch hands.'" Directly after she thought that, I switched hands, and the Lord began to move. What an amazing Holy Spirit! What a beautiful, childlike heart He is yearning to create in us. I learned then that following the Holy Spirit is about having a childlike trust in Him as a good Lord. The most simple act of obedience can change somebody's life forever. Jesus is like that, you know? Remember when He multiplied the fish and the bread. Before He did, He said, "Put them in groups of fifty and one hundred" (see Mark 6:39-40). Why? I don't know. Just because He wanted to. There are so many beautiful examples of the Lord asking us to do things that seem absolutely insignificant, and yet He uses them to be bridges that connect Heaven and earth in a second.

There is a passage in the Book of Acts that I absolutely love because I have found the principle it reveals to be true in daily life, in the ministry, and in a friendship with the Holy Spirit. The Bible shares an amazing truth with us in Acts 8:

Now an angel of the Lord said to Philip, "Go south to the road—the desert road—that goes down from Jerusalem to Gaza." So he started out, and on his way he met an Ethiopian eunuch, an important official in charge of all the treasury of the [queen]. This man had gone to Jerusalem to worship, and on his way home was sitting in his chariot reading the Book of Isaiah the prophet. The Spirit told Philip, "Go to that chariot and stay near it."

Then Philip ran up to the chariot and heard the man reading Isaiah the prophet. "Do you understand what you are reading?"

"How can I," he said, "unless someone explains it to me?" So he invited Philip to come up and sit with him.

This is the passage of the Scripture the eunuch was reading:

"He was led like a sheep to the slaughter, and as a lamb before its shearer is silent, so He did not open His mouth. In His humiliation He was deprived of justice. Who can speak of His descendants? For His life was taken from the earth."

The eunuch asked Philip, "Tell me, please, who is the prophet talking about, himself or someone else?" Then Philip began with that very passage of Scripture and told him the good news about Jesus.

As they traveled along the road, they came to some water and the eunuch said, "Look, here is water. What can stand in the way of my being baptized?" And he gave orders to stop the chariot. Then both Philip and the eunuch went down into the water and Philip baptized him. When they came up out of the water, the Spirit of the Lord suddenly took Philip away, and the eunuch did not see him again, but went on his way rejoicing (Acts 8:26-39 NIV).

Think of this for a moment: Why would the Bible go out of the way to highlight the fact that Philip ran to chariot in verse 30? Why didn't he walk? Why didn't he sprint? Why does it specifically say he ran? It is because a person who walks with the Holy Spirit understands the importance of instant obedience to the voice of God. Had Philip walked, he would've missed the chariot, which would've meant the eunuch would not have come to the Lord and would not have taken the Gospel back to Ethiopia. Ethiopia has been a Christian nation since the first century because Phillip decided to run when he heard the Holy Spirit speak to him. He knew that the Spirit was the Lord Himself. How powerful is the combination of the voice of the Spirit of the Lord and our obedience!

I've heard many people say, "I just don't hear His voice anymore. What should I do?" I'll often ask them, "What did He say to you the last time you heard Him?" And they'll tell me. I'll reply, "Did you do what He said?" They'll say, "No." My reply is, "Why would He continue to speak and trust you with more of His voice if you did not do what He said to do last time?" This walk with Him is not complicated. It is simple and childlike, yet full of depth and joy.

I remember the first time I stayed with a friend named Brian Garin. I was preaching at another friend's church in Baton Rouge, Louisiana. I woke up on Sunday morning to get ready to preach, and Brian had already been up praying. I did not know him very well at the time, but I had heard amazing things about his prophetic gift. Brian came to me in the morning and said, "I had a vision about you. I saw a man dressed in a camouflage outfit, and I heard a voice say, 'Be strict with him.'" And then he was shown in the encounter that there would be a demonic standoff in the meeting that morning. Well, as exciting as that probably sounds to you, it's not what you want to hear before you go preach. As powerful and as brave as we think we are, outside of the power of God, none of us want to deal with demons. I don't know about you, but battling with demons outside of the presence of God is not my idea of an enjoyable afternoon.

We went to the church, and I preached the first service. It was a good service, but it lacked the "It" factor, the glory of God. Between the first service and the evening service, the church decided to hold a prayer meeting. Well, if you want things to go up a notch in your church, I would highly recommend gathering the church to pray. When we walked into the building that evening, you could feel God in the room. It was an entirely different ballgame, and we all knew it. As I began to preach, signs and wonders started to flow and amazing miracles took place—there was no doubt that God was in the room. In fact, there was a visible glow over the crowd. I will never forget it as long as I live. Yet in the back of my mind, I often thought during the meeting, "Where is the standoff that Brian talked about?" Just before I dismissed the meeting, a large man—about 6'4", 260 pounds—walked down the center aisle with a very angry look on his face. He said, "I want to hear." This deaf man basically said in front of everybody, "Open my ears now." You talk about a challenge. In the natural, I have to admit I was a little intimidated and afraid, but I remembered that I did not make up the Bible; neither is it the Gospel according to Michael. This is Jesus' Gospel. This is His Kingdom. This is His work. So, I simply committed in my heart to do what Jesus told us to do—to *"lay hands on the sick, and they will recover"* (Mark 16:18).

I put my fingers in the man's ears and commanded his ears to open, and nothing happened. Again, I put my hands in his ears and screamed, "Open!" Nothing happened. Mind you, the entire church is watching this. I put my fingers back in his ears and said, "Open!" Nothing happened. The last time I did it, I looked into his eyes, and I saw that something was wrong. I instantly heard the Holy Spirit say to me, "He has a demon." I put my hand over his head into the air and rebuked the demon. When I did, his body began to contort. He began to bend backwards, his back attempting to become parallel with the ground while his feet remained on the ground. It was a sight to behold. He wanted to yield his body to the Lord, and this demon was fighting tooth and nail for it. Instantly, the man flew back onto the floor when

I rebuked the demon, and his eyes began to move in a crazy way. So the man lay there as the demon was fighting for His body and His soul. Brian walked up to me, and he said, "This is what I saw this morning in the vision. Remember, this a war. Be strict with this demon."

I did the only thing I knew to do: to see what the Holy Spirit would have me do next. After all, I had nothing to lose. The whole church was watching, and the man's ears were not opening. I remembered what Joy Dawson said to me when she was training me on how to deal with the demonic. Joy is one of the mothers of YWAM and has preached the Gospel in fifty-five nations of the world as a YWAM missionary. She was pivotal in forming the culture of YWAM in the early days regarding the character of God, the fear of the Lord, waiting on God, intercession, and a burden for the Gospel. For the last eight years, Joy has become a spiritual mother to me, and her words were ringing loud and clear in my spirit when I was dealing with this demon. I heard Joy say, "Use the name of Jesus, the Word of God, the blood of Jesus, and the power of the cross."

So I said out loud, "The Word of God says you've been rendered powerless, demon. The blood of Jesus is against you. The cross of Jesus is against you, and the name of Jesus is against you. I command you to come out." Immediately, the man started manifesting on the ground, hyperventilating, and shaking. His eyes were beet red. It was an intense moment, to say the least. Then I heard the faithful Holy Spirit say, "Remind him of the cross." And so, I reminded that demon of the power of the cross. When I did, I looked down at the man's face, and a single tear was streaming down his cheek. And I heard the Holy Spirit say, "Now command his ears to open." So, we stood the man up, and I said, "In the name of Jesus, I command your ears to open." And they opened in front of the whole place. I will never forget the look on the man's eyes when he began to hear. His wife ran up to him, and the first voice he heard was the voice of his wife. What a beautiful moment. It changed my life forever. I began to see that the Holy Spirit is not a tyrannical Lord who's merely telling us what to do for the sake of doing so, but He's a loving Lord who can be trusted; obeying His direction results in experiencing the goodness of God. I remember seeing the young people in the church watch this man's ears open. I don't think they'll ever forget that as long as they live. I'm so glad the Holy Spirit spoke to me that day. He is so wonderful.

My friend, you can trust the Holy Spirit even when He challenges you. The renewed mind begins to see a challenge as a bridge to greater breakthrough. The unrenewed mind sees a challenge from the Lord as a moment to fail. Our job is merely to obey. Once we obey the voice of the Holy Spirit, who is the Lord, He begins to take the matter into His own hands. I have seen this time and time again with healing miracles. My friend Paul Teske says, "Throw the pitch and watch God hit it." So simple but so profound. He goes onto say, "We often think, 'Well, what if I throw a bad pitch?'" His reply is, "You can throw any pitch you want to God. If He says, 'Throw it,' throw your best pitch, and God can hit a home run. If you throw it in the dirt, He can still hit a home run. You can throw it in the backstop, and He can still hit a home run with it. But if you don't throw the pitch, you will see significantly fewer home runs from God."

I pray you begin to trust the Lord. Trust His "yes" and trust His "no." How often do we not feel peace in our hearts when we're making a decision, and sometimes we see that as God's disapproval. Many times His "no" is an approval of our life. It shows His care and His compassion for us that He doesn't want us to make mistakes. A beautiful example of this is the Macedonian call that came to Paul the apostle. Just before Paul received a calling to go to Macedonia, he received a warning from the Holy Spirit not to go to Asia. Let's read beginning in verse 4:

Now while they were passing through the cities, they were delivering the decrees which had been decided upon by the apostles and elders who were in Jerusalem, for them to observe. So the churches were being strengthened in the faith, and were increasing in number daily. They passed through the Phrygian and Galatian region, having been forbidden by the Holy Spirit to speak the word in Asia; and after they came to Mysia, they were trying to go into Bithynia, and the Spirit of Jesus did not permit them; and passing by Mysia, they came to Troas. A vision appeared to Paul in the night: a man of Macedonia was standing and appealing to him, and saying, "Come over to Macedonia and help us." When he had seen the vision, immediately we sought to go into Macedonia, concluding that God had called us to preach the gospel to them (Acts 16:4-10 NASB).

This is a beautiful picture of the Holy Spirit functioning as our Lord. If He tells you not to do something, it is because He has something better for you to do with Him. Remember, in His will is a greater manifestation of His presence. His presence invites us into obedience, and obedience increases the measure of presence that we experience. So, in the will of God, as we listen carefully to the Holy Spirit and trust Him as our Lord, we are promised more presence, and more presence brings more satisfaction and more breakthrough.

THE SPIRIT OF WISDOM

The Holy Spirit is also called the Spirit of wisdom. Acts 6:8-10 says, *"And Stephen, full of grace and power, was performing great wonders and signs among the people. But some men from what was called the Synagogue of the Freedmen, including both Cyrenians and Alexandrians, and some from Cilicia and Asia, rose up and argued with Stephen. But they were unable to cope with the wisdom and the Spirit with which he was speaking"* (NASB). As you begin to walk in the Spirit and treasure His presence, wisdom will become yours. There's something I want you to understand: Wisdom is not something; it is Someone. It is the person of the Lord. In fact, the Bible says that "Jesus Christ is the wisdom of God" (see 1 Cor. 1:24).

Proverbs 2:2 says, *"Incline thine ear unto wisdom, and apply thine heart to understanding"* (KJV). This is simply telling us to give our ear to the voice and person of the Holy Spirit. Perhaps you're saying, "Wisdom is something, Michael. I don't agree with you. It can't be Someone." Proverbs 8:1 says, *"Does not wisdom call, and understanding lift up her voice?"* (NASB). Does a something call us? Of course not. Only a person calls. Proverbs 8:11 says, *"For wisdom is better than jewels; and all desirable things cannot compare with her"* (NASB). Moreover, listen to what the Scripture says in Proverbs 8:12-13: *"I, wisdom, dwell with prudence and I find knowledge and discretion. The fear of the Lord is to hate evil; pride and arrogance and the evil way and the perverted mouth, I hate"* (NASB). See, wisdom here is speaking as a person.

Again, the Bible says in Proverbs 8:14-21:

> *Counsel is mine and sound wisdom; I am understanding, power is mine. By me kings reign, and rulers decree justice. By me princes rule, and nobles, all who judge rightly. I love those who love me; and those who diligently seek me will find me. Riches and honor are with me, enduring wealth and righteousness. My fruit is better than gold, even pure gold, and my yield better than the choicest silver. I walk in the way of righteousness in the midst of the paths of justice, to endow those who love me with wealth, that I may fill their treasuries* (NASB).

By the language of the Scriptures here, does this sound like some inanimate object to you or some ethereal concept? No, Wisdom is certainly a person.

The Scripture goes on to say:

The Lord possessed me at the beginning of His way, before his works of old. From everlasting I was established, from the beginning, from the earliest times of the earth. When there were no depths I was brought forth, when there were no springs abounding with water. Before the mountains were settled, before the hills I was brought forth; while He had not yet made the earth and the fields, nor the first dust of the world. When He established the heavens, I was there. When He inscribed a circle on the face of deep, when He made firm the skies above, when the springs of the deep became fixed, when He set for the sea its boundary so that water would not transgress His command, when He marked out the foundations of the earth; then I was beside Him, as a master workman. [This is speaking of the presence of the Lord.] *And I was daily His delight, rejoicing always before Him. Rejoicing in the world, His earth, and having my delight in the sons of men. Now therefore, O sons, listen to me, for blessed are they who keep my ways. Heed instruction and be wise. Blessed is the man who listens to me, watching daily at my gates, waiting at my doorposts. For he who finds me finds life and obtains favor from the Lord. But he who sins against me injures himself; all those who hate me love death* (Prov. 8:22-36 NASB).

My friend, we do not sin against the thought or the concept of wisdom. We only sin against the person of God. If wisdom can be sinned against, it tells us that it is a person, the person of God Himself.

THE SPIRIT OF UNDERSTANDING

The Spirit of understanding is an awesome aspect of the Holy Spirit. While wisdom allows us into and unites us with the very thoughts and movement of the Spirit, the Spirit of understanding opens up His ways to us. The Holy Spirit begins to open the Word of God to us, and mysteries become available in a moment. Jesus expects us to understand

and comprehend His words. This will only come as a result of the Spirit of understanding moving in our lives. Jesus said, *"For the heart of this people has become dull, with their ears they scarcely hear, and they have closed their eyes, otherwise they would see with their eyes, hear with their ears, and understand with their heart and return, and I would heal them"* (Matt. 13:15 NASB). Notice the issue here is a heart issue, not merely a mind issue. The heart is absolutely connected with our thinking. Thus, it is connected to our ability to understand. The dull heart blinds us, deafens us, pushes us away from His presence, and keeps us emotionally sick. It is the desire of God to sensitize the heart first, then to trigger the rest of our spiritual senses. This is a spiritual issue that the Holy Spirit and He alone can fix. Once He touches the heart, He begins to open up the words of Jesus and we begin to understand the Word. Statements are no longer mere statements in the Scriptures. They become spiritual puzzle pieces that lead us into an encounter with God. As we begin to understand His ways, it becomes much easier to cooperate with Him, which leads to deeper fellowship. Without the Spirit of understanding, He can speak to us and we can leave having forgotten everything He said. The culture of Heaven becomes a reality to us as we discover the treasures of His Word. Authority is birthed in certain arenas because we see His ways clearly. Remember, a person is meant to be known, while a person's ways can be understood. It's like this: Wisdom sees the entire picture, the end from the beginning. Understanding helps us with the journey. Great visionaries often see Z from A due to wisdom flowing. They still need understanding to connect the other twenty-four letters that bridge the process. When the mind is renewed by the Spirit, it is evidence that the Spirit of understanding is beginning to operate in us.

THE SPIRIT OF KNOWLEDGE

Jesus knew the secrets of the hearts of men and women. We see this at work in the story of the woman at the well. He knew her thoughts and the details of her life. I believe the Spirit of knowledge opens us up to knowing God, to knowing His thoughts and His secrets. This was a marker in the life of the Lord. This is not the type of knowledge that "puffs up" (see 1 Cor. 8:1). Rather, it is the "knowing of God." First and foremost, this is connected to intimacy. God's desire is that we "know Him" instead of "facts." Once we begin to know the Holy Spirit, He begins to share His thoughts and feelings with us. Before He shares secrets with us, He wants us. Before we hear from Him, He wants us to meet Him...or at least to meet Him in the process. Nonetheless, His priority is knowing Him. Once we encounter the Holy Spirit as a person, we will discover that He has a lot to talk about. However, He will never exchange intimacy for information. For instance, words of knowledge (see 1 Cor. 12:8) should be a byproduct of the knowledge of Him. When John was called into His encounter in the Book of Revelation, he heard, *"Come up here, and I will show you..."* (Rev. 4:1). To make it simple, the Spirit of knowledge leads us into the knowing of God, which opens our hearts to know God's thoughts, which is meant to lead us into a deeper intimacy with God.

THE SPIRIT OF COUNSEL

The Bible says that the Lord is our counselor and only He has counsel. Proverbs 8:14 says, *"Counsel is mine, and sound wisdom: I am understanding; I have strength"* (KJV). Isaiah 9:6 declares, *"...His name shall be called Wonderful Counselor..."* (ESV). The Lord is certainly our counselor. Can you imagine that God is ready to give you advice to help you decide on pivotal issues, to warn you, and to instruct you? To take it a step further, we are invited by the Holy Spirit into the counsel of God. We literally have been given an open door to hear the conversations of the Trinity.

Jeremiah rebuked the false prophets of Israel for continually releasing false words of prophecy. He repeatedly said, "Repent because the

Babylonians are coming. God is going to judge Israel." Over and over, he warned them, with tears in his eyes, to come back to the Lord. And when he would release the Word of God to the king and the king's counselors, they were outraged by it. Other prophets stood up and said, "The Babylonians are not coming, we will not be judged. God is going to bless Israel," and Jeremiah rebuked them.

Take a look at Jeremiah 23:15-21:

> *Therefore thus saith the Lord of hosts concerning the prophets; Behold, I will feed them with wormwood, and make them drink the water of gall: for from the prophets of Jerusalem is profaneness gone forth into all the land. Thus saith the Lord of hosts, Hearken not unto the words of the prophets that prophesy unto you: they make you vain: they speak a vision of their own heart, and not out of the mouth of the Lord. They say still unto them that despise Me, The Lord hath said, Ye shall have peace; and they say unto every one that walketh after the imagination of his own heart, No evil shall come upon you. For who hath stood in the counsel of the Lord, and hath perceived and heard His word? Who hath marked His word, and heard it? Behold, a whirlwind of the Lord is gone forth in fury, even a grievous whirlwind: it shall fall grievously upon the head of the wicked. The anger of the Lord shall not return, until He has executed, and till He has performed the thoughts of His heart: in the latter days ye shall consider it perfectly. I have not sent these prophets, yet they ran: I have not spoken to them, yet they prophesied* (KJV).

That is an amazing passage. In other words, the false prophets were false because they had not stood in the counsel of the Lord. They had not given God the time to lift their souls into the heavenly places so that they would be privy to the conversations of God. They spoke on their own accord because the Spirit of counsel was not flowing in their lives. Remember, Jesus said, "The Holy Spirit would not speak of Himself, but He will tell us of everything He hears that comes from the Father and the Son" (see John 16:13). As you listen to the Holy Spirit, you are listening to the will of the Father that is administrated by the Son through the voice of the Holy Spirit. To be clear, to receive the counsel of the Holy Spirit is to receive the counsel of the Godhead. We are literally invited into the plans of God. God has a plan for America. God has a plan for the nations of the world. God has a plan for every stay-at-home mom in the world. He has a plan for your pastor, and He has a plan for your children. He has a plan for everything and everyone, and God wants to share that plan with us. God has a perfect plan for every service, every Bible study, and every soccer game.

When the Spirit of counsel is invited in through a hungry, yielded heart, God begins to speak to us and share His plans with us. This is so precious for many reasons. Can you believe that God is eager to share His dearest and deepest feelings with you, His friend? The Spirit of counsel opens your ears to the Mighty Counselor.

I have learned that it is much easier to join what God is already doing than to attempt to get God to bless what I am doing. Early on in my ministry days, this was a real struggle for me. There was so much that I wanted to see happen in the meetings, and they were all wonderful ambitions. They were all biblical. I would strive and strive, and nothing would happen. I so badly wanted the sick to be healed. I wanted revival with every fiber of my being. I wanted the fire of God to sweep through our meetings. And to be honest, those things rarely happened. Finally, I realized that instead of trying to twist God's arm, I could simply wait and listen to Him. Once I sensed, saw, heard, or felt what He was doing, I learned simply to yield to that plan. That combination became a combustible reward. The power of God was released in those services. What was once dead quickly came to life. I realized that God had a plan for every moment of every day. Saying "yes" to that plan was the bridge that connected Heaven and Earth in the moment. Once that connection took place, I simply had to hold on for the ride.

I'll never forget telling Heidi Baker, "Heidi, I struggled for so many years, and then one day I sensed that Jesus just wanted to walk into our meetings—that if I could figure out a way to allure Him to walk through the services, He would come. So I just began to worship and wait, Heidi, and He came and did everything so much better, so much more powerfully." Heidi looked at me with a smile, and she said, "That's it. Isn't it way better that way?" Experiencing the Spirit of counsel leads us into an awesome realm called the Spirit of might.

THE SPIRIT OF MIGHT

The Spirit of might is awesome. There are times in our lives where we need breakthrough, we need God to do the impossible. Miracles are a vital part of our lives as Christians. We need miracles, and the world needs miracles. The Spirit of might is so needed in the Church today, and I believe God wants to pour it out in a huge way. Might is great strength, force, or power. Deuteronomy 3:24 says, *"O Lord God, Thou hast begun to shew Thy servant Thy greatness, and Thy mighty hand: for what God is there in heaven or in earth, that can do according to Thy works, and according to Thy might?"* (KJV). Let's remember, in our own strength, we have no might. Psalm 24:8 says, *"Who is this King of glory? The Lord strong and mighty, the Lord mighty in battle."* The source of power and might is God Himself. Job 12:13 declares, *"With Him are wisdom and might..."* (NASB).

Have you ever pondered the incredible victory that Jesus accomplished on the cross and through His resurrection? Just think for a moment about how when Jesus died, He descended into the underworld and took captivity captive. The Bible goes on to say that He embarrassed the devil himself. This side of Jesus is one of my favorites. I love the fact that

He's strong and mighty. Can you picture Him down there enforcing His greatness and victory? How about the Jesus who turned over the money tables? Or how about the Jesus who cast out demons with a spoken word? Of course we love the One who puts children on His knee and blesses them with His hand, but I love the Lion as much as I love the Lamb. Jeremiah 32:18-19 says, *"...the Great, the Mighty God, the Lord of hosts, is His name, great in counsel, and mighty in work..."* (KJV). Daniel describes Him this way in Daniel 2:20: *"Blessed be the name of God forever and ever, to whom belong wisdom and might"* (ESV).

It's important we understand that there's nothing difficult for the Lord. There are no huge miracles or small miracles in the Kingdom. To God, everything is done, and everything is easy. At the cross, Jesus paid the price for every stubbed toe and every cancerous tumor. He purchased every healing and every miracle for every person that has ever lived. Every allergy and every dead body waiting to be raised, and everything in between, have been paid for by Jesus Himself. Yet the Bible does say in Acts 19:11 that *"God wrought special miracles by the hands of Paul"* (KJV).

I believe there are different realms as it pertains to us in the miraculous and the Spirit of might. In other words, to God nothing is difficult because He has paid for everything. He's creator of all things. When God speaks, it is completed. The question is, how do we walk in and experience what is already in our account? Well, there are many answers, but at the end of the day, I believe surrender and hunger are two of the greatest keys we could ever possess in accessing the Spirit of might, the Holy Spirit Himself.

Samson understood the Spirit of might after running miles carrying a gate to a city. Elijah knew the Spirit of might as he lived on no food for forty days and journeyed, and preached, and ministered. Paul knew the Spirit of might as he shook off a viper that bit him in the hand. Jesus understood the Spirit of might when all were healed in entire cities and villages. Just imagine—Jesus could cast a devil out of somebody in an entirely different city just through the spoken word. This is the Spirit of might in operation. It basically makes you a super Christian, where nothing is impossible. Jesus showed us the Spirit of might when He walked on water and multiplied bread and fish. The Holy Spirit will change you. The Holy Spirit will make you into a real man or woman of God. Your limitations will die when the Spirit of might touches your life.

When you think of the revivalists and the great voice of the healing movement, you think of Oral Roberts laying hands on ten thousand people in one night, many being healed as his hands touched them. Think of Kathryn Kuhlman, this frail, old woman traveling from city to city, preaching her heart out and ministering to the sick. Think of Maria Woodworth-Etter continuing in her ministry after losing five of her children to disease. As she would pull into a town, people would fall under the power a mile in each direction. How could this happen? The Holy Spirit, the Spirit of might. He takes your weakness and hides it in Himself. He then uses that weakness as space to fill you with His power.

How badly we need the Spirit of might today! Hospitals are fuller than ever. Nations around the world are waiting to hear the Gospel. Governments need to see miracles. Presidents and prime ministers have sick family members and their money cannot save them, yet they're looking for somebody or something to deliver them. Churches are hungry for the genuine presence of God. Sickness stands and mocks the promises of God. All the while Jesus is waiting for somebody's surrender to become the torch and the ignition for the Spirit of might to be on display. The Holy Spirit is more ready than we could ever be. He's ready to touch the world. He's ready to enforce what Jesus prayed for. What is He looking for? A life that recognizes its own weakness; somebody who says to themselves and to God, "I need You. I may not have much to give You, but if I get You, I get everything. Here I am, Lord. Touch me."

I pray that like Paul in Romans 15:19, many will say of our lives, *"Through mighty signs and wonders, by the power of the Spirit of God... [we] have fully preached the gospel of Christ"* (KJV). And so, this is my prayer for you—it's actually a Scripture that I would like to speak over you as you read this: *"Finally, my brethren, be strong in the Lord, and in the power of His might"* (Eph. 6:10 KJV).

THE SPIRIT OF THE FEAR OF THE LORD

In 2008, I was privileged to be approached by one of the greatest women of God on planet Earth. Her name is Joy Dawson. I was assisting my father-in-law in those days. She walked up to me in a healing service in Long Beach, California, and said, "I would love to speak to you. I really believe that you and I are supposed to connect. When you have time, and only when you have time, would you come to my seat and chat with me a bit?" I was absolutely shocked that Joy Dawson had approached me. You have to understand, I grew up watching her on television, I had watched her teach, and she was a real hero to our family. Joy carries a real presence about her.

So, I walked up to Joy's seat, squatted down, and for the first time had an in-depth conversation with her and her husband, Jim. Jim has gone on to be with the Lord now, and I miss him dearly. He was always in a wonderful mood, ready to laugh, and full of humility. At the end of the conversation, Joy said to me, "Here's my phone number. Be sure to give me a call. I would like to begin speaking with you." And so, we scheduled a call, and Joy and I spoke for the first time by telephone. The conversation lasted approximately two hours. It was riveting and full of God. I will never forget it.

Beginning with my mother, women of God have influenced my life in an amazing way. As you know, Kathryn Kuhlman, Basilea Schlink, Aimee Semple McPherson, and Maria Woodworth-Etter have all deeply impacted my life. I would have to put Joy Dawson on that list as well. She has been a loving, faithful, truthful, and loyal friend to me for the last eight years.

That phone call was my introduction to the Spirit of the fear of the Lord. Joy carried it all over here, and it flowed from her mouth. The Bible says, *"The fear of the Lord is the beginning of wisdom"* (Prov. 9:10). This implies that without the fear of the Lord, we walk in foolishness and blindness before God. Our eyes are unable to see who He is. It is literally the gateway to the vision of God. The Bible says that Jesus was anointed with the Spirit of the fear of the Lord (see Isa. 11:2). The fear of the Lord is to be simply in awe of God. It is an awe that draws us to the Lord. It is an awe that creates a dependence on the Lord. The Bible says that those who fear the Lord have lips that are free from deceit (see Ps. 34:13). As Joy would say, this does not only mean that we tell the truth but that we tell all of the truth all of the time. There are no exaggerations or white lies in the fear of the Lord. It is an aware-ness that God is always there, always listening, and always watching. It is an absolute obsession with His presence and the understanding that we have His attention. As we grow in the fear of the Lord, we grow in wisdom. We begin to see the Lord for who He is. We understand that He is not just a lamb but is also a lion. That He is alpha and omega. That He is love and fire. A sobriety comes into our lives as we realize that we will give an account for everything done in this body, as Paul said in Second Corinthians 5:10.

When the fear of the Lord touches you, you begin to see the abso-lute holiness of the Lord. I believe this is what happened to John the beloved on the island of Patmos when he saw the resurrected Jesus in Revelation 1. This is why he fell dead at His feet. He saw into the Lord in a way that he had never seen before. This happened on the Mount of Transfiguration when Peter, John, and James were afraid by what they saw: Jesus emitting flashes of lightning from His body, the cloud of the Holy Spirit hovering above them, the fire within the cloud, and the voice of the Father. What a scene as they encountered the fear of the Lord. Moses had this experience on Mount Sinai as he beheld the Ancient of Days, amazed by the fire that engulfed the entire mountain.

Perhaps you're asking, "Then why would the Scripture tell us to approach the throne of grace boldly?" (see Heb. 4:16; Eph. 3:12). Let me explain what I mean by the word *fear*. As God moves into the scene and expresses Himself, our humanity realizes His absolute greatness. It is in holy experiences like this where we realize that God is everything, that He is pure and holy, and that He is absolute light with no darkness, or shadow, or turning (see James 1:17). While we are incredibly aware of His love for us, we also realize that He holds our breath in His hand and that we are but dust.

To be honest, I want a God whom I fear this way. I want a Jesus who is holy. I love the fact that He has eyes of fire and rod in His hand. I love the fact that He's righteous and just. Understanding this makes me more amazed at the fact that this amazing God, who has no beginning and no end, would come and die for me. The Holy Spirit gives us the fear of the Lord. In fact, Jesus delighted in the fear of the Lord (see Isa. 11:3). Jesus Himself was completely awestruck by the absolute holiness of His Father. How much more, then, should we!

I'm privileged to minister and have a relationship with many denominations and streams. I have preached to young and old, Baptists and Pentecostals, Catholics and Methodists, and everything in between. There's something that has been concerning me as of late. It is the thought that because of God's amazing grace, we no longer need the fear of the Lord. Proof that grace has touched your life is the presence of the fear of the Lord on your life. The Bible says that grace and truth come through Jesus (see John 1:17). In other words, they literally flow through the person of Jesus. He is the source and the means by which grace and truth come to our lives. Therefore, we should become more and more like Jesus every day if we are experiencing His grace.

The ancient fathers of the church used to say this about somebody who carried the glory of God: "He has been graced with the Holy Spirit." In other words, grace was not so much a free pass to do whatever you want, but it was the power that bathed and wrapped God's friends in the Holy Spirit. To put it quite simply, if you want to know that grace is flowing and winning in your life, you should be more like Jesus today than you were yesterday.

The fear of the Lord will challenge you. God will test you to see if you, like Jesus, will delight in the fear of the Lord. Charles Spurgeon says, "You are who you are when nobody is watching." In other words, if you want to know the real you, the real you is the one who lives when nobody is watching. I've had God challenge me so many times in private with what might look like small things—like putting a shopping cart back that's out in the middle of a parking lot, or picking up a piece of garbage, or giving a poor person a few dollars. Sometimes He challenges me to pick up somebody's tab in a restaurant. Maybe you're asking, "What's that got to do with the fear of the Lord?" Everything! When His voice outweighs the opinions of men and your own opinions, you are beginning to walk in the fear of the Lord. The beauty of this is that God will begin to open up the treasure of wisdom as He sees that we can be trusted with the fear of the Lord. His wisdom is so precious that it must fall into the lives of those who are trustworthy and have shown Him that they value Him above all else. Character carries gifting and revelation. The fear of the Lord forges character in our lives. Without the Holy Spirit it is impossible to have the fear of the Lord, but with Him it is your promise.

Chapter Thirteen

WINE

There's a beautiful story in the Scriptures of a Jewish man who is traveling on a road, and on his way he is beaten up, hurt badly, robbed, and ends up in really bad shape. The first two people that go by decide not to help him, but then a Samaritan comes by, sees him, and the Bible says he does something amazing. He pours wine and oil on his wounds (see Luke 10:25-37).

The Holy Spirit is referred to as wine in the Scriptures. Paul actually makes a comparison by saying, *"Be not drunk with wine…but be filled with the Spirit"* (Eph. 5:18 KJV). Wine is interesting because it possesses many qualities that are very similar to those of the Holy Spirit. First of all, wine is aged. The best wine is aged wine.

You remember the story of the wedding in Cana? It was the setting for Jesus' first miracle. I love this story for so many reasons. First and foremost, I love it because it involves Jesus. I love anything that involves Him. Secondly, it's a beautiful picture of His relationship with His mother and of the beautiful, natural nature of Jesus. He was not too spiritual to attend a wedding and celebrate with those who are celebrating.

Mary comes to the Lord because there is a problem at the wedding. They had run out of wine. And so, the master of the ceremony was a bit stressed. Mary came to the Lord and told Him. After dialoguing with Mary and after a little back-and-forth with His mother, Jesus gave direction, and He told the servants, "Fill up the vessels with water" (see John 2:7). And they filled up the vessels with water, and by the power of the Holy Spirit, that water was turned into wine. Everyone began to drink after the miracle took place. And the people said, "You have saved the best wine for last. Typically, the best wine is first, but you saved the best for last" (see John 2:10).

Isn't this a picture of the Holy Spirit in so many different ways? It is an especially beautiful picture of the way of the Holy Spirit. As amazing as Pentecost was, for instance, He promises that the latter will be greater than the former—that the reign, that the glory of the latter house would be greater than that of the former house (see Hag. 2:9). And the way of the Holy Spirit is always to multiply Himself.

The river of God that we see in Ezekiel 47, it goes from shallow to deep. That is always the progression of the Lord. Now, that's not to say that every person who is born again continues to go deeper and deeper. It's only to say that the will of God is that we go deeper and deeper. If we start off shallow, grow into depth, and then move into the shallows again, it is not because of the Lord. God's way is increase. Even when He prunes, it's so that we might bear more fruit. So it's not a shock to us that Jesus waited until the very end of the wedding not only to turn water into wine, but also to make sure that it was much better than the best wine man could offer at the beginning of the wedding. It's also important for us to notice and understand that the Lord waited until they ran out of their own wine, which was man-made. This would cause them to ask for the wine that comes from Jesus, the Holy Spirit.

And this is what the Lord is wanting from us. He's wanting us to realize that anything that's man-made, anything that finds its origin in the flesh, while it might look good and taste good, it's not eternal; it runs out. The wine that comes from Heaven, it never runs out.

David said it this way: "My cup runs over" (see Ps. 23:5). The Greek translation from the Septuagint would say it this way: "I am intoxicated with wine from your cup." Even in the Old Covenant, David knew, because by the Spirit he had seen the beauty of the New Covenant, that there was a beautiful secret, that the blessing of the New Covenant was this: God would love in men. That God the Holy Spirit would make His home in our bodies, and that we would no longer have to go to the temple to find Him but that our bodies would become the house of God. That deep within us we could always drink of the wine of the Holy Spirit.

What Does the Wine of the Spirit Do?

First of all, that wine was used in the story of the Good Samaritan to disinfect and to bring healing to the wounds of the man who was hurt so badly. The oil would cover and protect the wound and cause the wound to begin closing. It would keep infection from setting in long term. It would become a calming agent to the wound. But the initial application would have been the wine because alcohol disinfects. Now, this is a picture of the blood of Jesus, no doubt, but it is also a picture of the wine of the Holy Spirit and His work. The Holy Spirit not only protects us and empowers us, but He also disinfects us. He is actually the One who brings and carries the benefits of the blood of Jesus to our lives. That's what the Bible teaches—that the blessings of Abraham have come to us by the Spirit (see Gal. 3:14). In fact, the blood and the Spirit and water, the Bible says, work together; they bear witness in Heaven and on earth (see 1 John 5:8). It is the same today. The Holy

Spirit and the power of the blood, they work in perfect harmony. In fact, the Bible says that it was through the blood of Jesus that the Holy Spirit raised Jesus from the dead (see Heb. 13:20).

Next, when wine is consumed in the Spirit and we are filled with the Spirit, we experience what David called "an intoxication." There is a beautiful drunkenness in the Holy Spirit. This is full of joy, full of peace. There is a holy inebriation that comes to those who are constantly beholding the Lord. The early saints of old talked about this. The 120 in the upper room on the day of Pentecost were called drunkards because of the work of the Holy Spirit. Some believe that this is because they spoke in tongues, but that is not the case. Let me ask you a simple question: If your friend, who spoke perfect English and only perfect English, all of a sudden began to speak perfect Portuguese, would you attribute to that to drinking alcohol? No. In fact, your conclusion would be the exact opposite. You wouldn't say, "You must be drunk." You would say, "You're a genius."

So why were they called drunkards? It was because of the effect that the Holy Spirit was having on them, the joy that He was producing in their souls, the way that they were declaring the Word of the Lord in the native tongues of all who were listening. You see, it's not just what we preach, but how we preach it. It's what oozes out of us when we speak. The wine of Heaven brings a happiness and a peace that nothing else can. I believe that this is one of the gifts from the Lord that helps us experience the following Scripture: "We are in the world but not of the world" (see John 17:14). In other words, our bodies are planted here on earth. Our minds are dealing with both worlds; but deep in our spirit, the new wine of Heaven begins to flow, and we receive this heavenly drink that causes us to lose sight of all that holds us. All the fear and all the worry that the world offers begin to dissipate, and we begin to live a true heavenly life.

Now, any good wine is also hidden and covered. *This speaks of value.* I've been in caves in Italy that hold hundreds of bottles of wine. The reason they're hidden down there is because they're valuable. While the Holy Spirit is given to all who love Jesus, the new wine of Heaven is not experienced by all Christians. This is because there is a side of the Lord that causes Him to hide Himself. In fact, the Bible says in the Book of Isaiah, "I am the Lord who hideth" (see Isa. 45:15). There is this side of God because of His supreme value, which demands that we seek Him. As those wine bottles hide in those dark caves, so there are aspects of the Holy Spirit that we can find only in solitude by digging into the depths of His heart. Yet as we dig and walk and trust and listen into areas that few have, we can count on the Holy Spirit to unlock the wine of Heaven that's been covered and aged for years.

Chapter Fourteen

FIRE

The Holy Spirit is so fun and colorful. There are so many facets to His nature. Yes, He's intertwined with the Father and the Son, but He has qualities of His own that are also beautiful. This is the mystery of the Trinity—that all of His qualities belong to the Father and Son, yet He has a very specific personality Himself. We see this in the different forms in which He reveals Himself in the Bible. The Bible says, "He came as a dove," but He is not a dove. He appeared as a burning bush, but He is not a bush. He is spoken about as being a wind, but there is so much more to Him than being a wind. The point is this: These beautiful pictures are descriptions of His nature, and He wants you to get to know Him.

Let's talk about the Holy Spirit as fire. John the Baptist said, "There's one coming after me who will baptize you in the Holy Spirit and fire, whose sandals I am not worthy to unloose" (see Matt. 3:11; Luke 3:16). Again, we see in Exodus chapter 3 that Moses encounters a bush that would not burn, and from that bush there was a fire. As the children of Israel walked through the wilderness for forty years, a pillar of fire went before them and led them through the dark night of their journey to the Promised Land. That fire was not only a light but also a warmth that would protect them, keep predators away, and let the nations of the world know that although they were in the wilderness, they still belonged to God. He was their light and their heat.

When Moses dedicated the tabernacle, God showed His approval by descending as fire on the altar, and that fire never went out. Solomon fulfilled the dream of his father and through the wisdom of God built the temple and followed the blueprint that David handed down to him. After assembling Israel, the Levites, the musicians, the beautiful choir, the different artifacts, and the pieces of the holy temple, Solomon dedicated it to the Lord, and the Lord appeared, descended as fire, and consumed the sacrifice.

Around God's throne is fire. In front of Him is a sea of glass with fire inside of it. That fire is the Holy Spirit. What a picture John was painting for those who came to be baptized by him when he said, "One's coming after me who will baptize you in the Holy Spirit and fire" (see Matt. 3:11; Luke 3:16). Again, the Bible says, *"Our God is a consuming fire"* (Heb. 12:29). It's interesting that John chose to introduce Jesus as the baptizer in the Holy Spirit and fire while John was baptizing people himself in water. It was the perfect opportunity to give an illustrated sermon.

In every baptism, there are a few things we need to understand regarding God's way of baptizing. There is the baptizer, there is the baptizee, there is the element that we're baptized into, and then there is the result or fruit of the baptism. In John's baptism, John was the baptizer, the people that came to him were the baptizees, the element was water, and the fruit of that baptism was repentance. This is why John said that we were to show the fruit of repentance to work the works of repentance (see Matt. 3:8). In the baptism of the Holy Spirit and fire, the baptizer is Jesus, the baptizees are you and me, the element is the Holy Spirit and fire, and the fruit is this: "You will become witnesses unto Me" (see Acts 1:8).

So, as John stood at the banks and took people who came to him and plunged them into the waters of the Jordan, so Jesus takes us as we come to Him and plunges us into the depths of the river of God, a river of presence and fire. We literally come out dripping with the very substance of God Himself.

Now, God is not just a flame. He is not a tiny little candle hoping to be seen. No, the Lord is a real fire. To be even more precise, He is a certain type of fire: He is a consuming fire. The fire of the Holy Spirit protects us, warms us, illuminates us, but it also burns up all that is in us that is not of God. In other words, when the Holy Spirit is done burning in us, only He and His presence remain.

We need fire again. We need real Holy Spirit fire. Our generation is tired of sitting through services that are perfectly planned, perfectly calm, perfectly directed by men and women, yet leave the sinner a sinner, leave the backslider backslidden, and leave those sick and suffering in their disease. We need real fire again.

THE MAGNET OF THE CROSS

I believe in impartation. In fact, I'm going to talk about that later in the book. I believe in serving and honoring those who have gone before us. This is a precious and vital truth in growing in the Lord and influence on the earth. I believe in surrounding ourselves with men and women who have achieved more and experienced more in the Lord than we have. I have many of those people in my own life. While I do believe that mantles can be transferred and that impartation can take place, I have also seen many people take their eyes off Jesus because they're so focused on a man's mantle.

Let's have a look at the life of Jesus and see the mantle that He chose. The Bible says that on the night He was betrayed, He took the cup and shared the Last Supper with His disciples. When they were through celebrating the Passover, the Scripture says that Jesus took off His cloak, laid it down, took a rag, and girded Himself with it (see John 13:4). This is incredibly powerful language. In those days, what you wore told the world who you were and what you did. Your clothing was a picture of your status in society. Jesus was a rabbi; therefore, He wore a rabbi's clothing. But here in this holy moment, He takes His garment off and wears a rag. This is amazing. He was not merely saying, "I am here to serve and to wash feet," though that is amazing in itself. He was saying, "I am here to be a servant." You see, being and doing something once are completely different. And so, Jesus took off His mantle of honor, took on the nature of a servant, and began to wash the feet of His disciples.

What was the next mantle that Jesus sought? I would venture to say you've never heard what you're about to read. Jesus endured the cross with joy and put the cross on His back as a mantle. He wore a mantle of wood—a mantle that marked Him as a reject of society and as a criminal. And today, I can say unequivocally that beyond the mantles you seek, that Somebody Else has walked in power and miracles. We see miracles in every meeting, and I will never shortchange that. But more than any mantle of man that you need, we all need to wear the mantle of the cross.

This is a heavy mantle. It's a mantle whose weight you feel. It's not a burden, but it's a holy weight that marks you before the heavens and the world, that notifies demonic powers that you are following the path of Jesus. As Madame Guyon said, "God gives us the cross, and the cross gives us God."[1] When you say, "Jesus, I will carry my cross" and obey His command that *if any man will come after Me, let him deny himself, and take up his cross daily, and follow Me*" (Luke 9:23 KJV), the moment you do that—the moment you deny self and put a cross on your back—every devil in hell will know something: *This man belongs to God.* It's a clear announcement to the unseen world that you are not your own.

What we often forget to realize is that once that cross is embedded into your nature and you wear it gladly, it becomes more than a cross. It becomes an altar. That's right, the cross is an altar. That's why the altar of sacrifice in the tabernacle was in the shape of a cross. It's because instead of a lamb being slaughtered every day, one day the Lamb of God would be slaughtered on that cross. And so, the cross is Heaven's altar. Instead of the blood of animals, the blood of Jesus runs down that cross. The cross becomes an altar in the eyes of Heaven.

Do you remember what falls on the altar? Can you remember how God gives His "amen" upon an altar? It's by sending fire. And so, as you place the cross on your back, it becomes a magnet for the fire of the Holy Spirit.

NOTE

1. Madame Guyon, *Experiencing Union with God through Inner Prayer & The Way and Results of Union with God* (Orlando, FL: Bridge-Logos, 2001), 42.

Chapter Fifteen

OIL

My wife, Jessica, is really into health. I must say, so am I. For example, Jessica never puts the synthetic bug spray on our kids. We love to be outdoors. Playing golf and fishing are our favorite pastimes. In Florida, bugs are a big deal. They are literally everywhere. The mosquitoes down here do a lot more than fly by. They bite you and bite you again. They have a way of making you want to go crazy. So, we have to lather ourselves with bug spray. We use a healthy, organic alternative. I have to admit, it does work. There is only one issue: It leaves you feeling a little oily. Oil is the base substance for the bug sprays we use. While the oily spray does repel most of the bugs, some are so committed to sucking our blood that they fly straight into the oil. Guess what? They die when they land.

This is so much like the anointing of the Holy Spirit on our lives. Yes, there are many counterfeit alternatives out there. There are actually church conferences and books out there that teach you how to grow your ministry systematically but don't mention a relationship with the

Holy Spirit. They will tell you how your services should be scheduled, but they don't reference bathing in the oil of God so that He can flow through you in the meeting. Yes, just as there are many synthetic bug sprays out there that work in the short term but cause harm in the long term, there are synthetic solutions to ministry.

We must choose daily to contend for the authentic life in the Holy Spirit, which Jesus modeled for us. Success is loving Jesus, not growing in numbers. Growth should be a byproduct of genuine union with the Holy Spirit. Reject the synthetic, man-made methods by yielding to God's voice in your life.

Just as the genuine oil protects me and my children from bugs, so the Holy Spirit protects us from the powers of hell. In the bug repellant, it is the smell of the oil and the spices that keeps the bugs away. The same is true in the spiritual life. It is the fragrance of Jesus in the oil of the Spirit that repels the attacks of the enemy. The devil literally hates the presence of the Holy Spirit. However, if an attack does get through to us (just as there are bugs that occasionally reach our skin despite the natural bug spray), the Holy Spirit—that Pure Oil—will stop it in its tracks. I love to see the devil get smoked. I really do.

I believe the greatest protection we could ever have is the presence of God Himself wrapping us like a cloak.

PROTECTION FROM JUDGMENT

There is a greater judgment for those who teach the Scriptures (see James 3:1). I believe we must take our callings seriously and live a holy life. The world is yearning for a true picture of Jesus. Beryl Moore said, "Jesus put a face on the Father, and we put a face on Jesus to the world." That is beautiful! I would add only a little something to that beautiful statement. I'd say it this way: Jesus put a face on the Father, and the Holy Spirit puts Jesus' face on ours. Let's remember that we are held to a higher standard if we are teaching people the Scriptures. To be honest, my heart breaks to see so many young leaders accepting sin in hopes of reaching more people. God doesn't need our compromise to reach the lost. He needs our surrender. We need some of the old-time fire swagger again. I know I need to be bathed in love and grace. I've discovered the more that God's love has bathed me, the more I hate the devil and sin. Sin destroys people, and I hate that.

Aaron

I will never forget a powerful conversation I had with my father-in-law one night. We were discussing the Holy Spirit's presence in and anointing on our lives and how precious He is. I really couldn't imagine a day without Him—life would be hell on earth. In fact, it wouldn't be life at all.

My father-in-law said to me, "Just think, when God judged Miriam for speaking against Moses, He didn't touch Aaron. Aaron did the same thing she did."

They both criticized Moses for marrying an Ethiopian woman. Then, for their grand mistake, they said, "Are you the only one who hears from God?" (see Num. 12:2). They hadn't crossed the line until they mentioned Moses' position before God. I don't believe they would have angered the Lord if they had just continued the conversation regarding the Ethiopian woman. But the moment they invaded Moses' relationship with God and compared themselves to Moses spiritually, they entered a new realm. They left the territory of a family discussion and entered the realm of Kingdom.

God would not have it. So, He said, "With you I speak in mysteries and riddles, but with Moses I speak face to face" (see Num. 12:8). In other words, "Back off, Aaron and Miriam. He may be your brother, but He is My son. I made him and have walked with him. I have acquaintances, and I have friends. Moses is My friend. He's much closer to Me than you are. Since you have decided to come against My friend and to come between Me and him, I need to make a point to all of Israel." As we know, nothing happened to Aaron, but Miriam was struck with leprosy. Why? It's because of the anointing oil that covered Aaron and his garments. God smelled the fragrance that rested on Aaron, the high priest, who was a picture of Jesus and His nature. You see, when God saw Aaron, He saw a prophetic picture of Jesus, our High Priest. When He looked at Aaron's garments and saw the oil, He saw the anointing of the Holy Spirit resting on His Son. So, God did not touch Aaron, because he was protected by oil and the very fragrance of Jesus. While I am not saying that we can assume that God will be blind to our willful sin, there is no doubt that He has great patience and grace for those who have been anointed with Heaven's oil, the Holy Spirit.

David

Something that is very important to me, my family, and our ministry at Jesus Image is honor. To us, it's non-negotiable. We believe this is a revelation that is vital in the Kingdom. Because of God's blessing on our ministry, I'm often asked, "How can you associate with this person? How can you risk your brand by even being linked with so-and-so? They have messed up. They have failed. You don't agree with all they do and say. They are going to hurt you in the long run. If you do decide to remain in a friendship with them, you should do it secretly. If they have impacted your life, just tell people privately. Don't ever do it publicly." The thought of that type of heart literally makes me nauseated. To be honest, it sounds a lot like the political arena. A few years back, I remember Bill Johnson telling me, "There are two spirits that you will have to confront and deal with: the political spirit and the religious spirit." How right he was. The political spirit says, "Even though God has blessed your life and you have been a blessing to me, I can't publicly be associated with you because you have failed in your life." Sorry to be so frank, but how gross is that? What have we become when we throw fathers and mothers in God to the wayside because of their bad decisions? I would rather go back to the life of a professional golfer than to be bound to the opinions of men while serving Jesus.

Let's have a look at David and see what God's opinion was of him. Did you know that David was anointed three times: once as a shepherd boy (possibly at the age of twelve) so that he could kill Goliath, another time as king of Judah, and lastly as king of Israel. David was very familiar with the precious oil—the presence of the Holy Spirit. His first anointing, given by Samuel while he tended to his sheep, would change his life forever. His private battle-tested skills would now go public and take center stage before all of Israel. Oh yes, he knew the effect that the oil had on his life. Of course he sensed something different on him. Who was it that gave David the boldness to challenge Goliath before two nations? Where did the certainty come from that he would not only kill Goliath, but also cut off Goliath's head and even kill Goliath's brothers? Remember, he took five smooth stones from the brook. Goliath had four brothers, and God never does anything by chance. What carried that rock directly into Goliath's forehead? Was David really that good? My friend, the answer to all of the above is the presence of the Spirit that rested on David once the oil was poured on him by Samuel, God's prophet.

After years of testing and turmoil, David would eventually be king of Judah and Israel. Yet, David failed—many times and in many ways. He was an adulterer, a murderer, a horrible friend, a deceiver, prideful, self-exalting, and greedy. In fact, in comparison to the people who often receive our scorn, David was the worst offender. Did God punish David? Yes, He did. He punished him harshly, but He didn't throw him away. Why? First and foremost, because David repented. It was also because he wore the oil. The oil reminded God that David was the Lord's and that one day, the Eternal King would take His eternal throne as the offspring of David.

Given David's many failures, should we erase his successes and heart for the Lord? Should we eliminate First and Second Samuel eternally from the Scriptures? How about the Book of Psalms? What about Jesus' title as Son of David? Of course not! Why must David remain honored before us? It's because God chose him. God raised him up. God poured His oil on him. If he is good enough for God, he should be good enough for us.

Solomon

Solomon was quite a person. What gifting! What wisdom! What a human being! Let's have a look at his resume for a moment:

- He is born to David and Bathsheba.

- He receives the promise that he will be king of Israel.

- He is David's beloved son.

- God Himself appears to him and asks him what he wants.

- He becomes the wisest man in history next to Jesus.

- He becomes the richest man in history.

- He becomes probably the greatest peacekeeper the world has ever known.

- He writes the Book of Proverbs, Song of Solomon, and Ecclesiastes.

- He is named in First Kings, Second Kings, First Chronicles, Second Chronicles, Second Samuel, Matthew, Luke, Nehemiah, and Acts.

- He builds Israel's first temple.

Oh yeah, one more thing: he was anointed with oil by Zadok the priest. Not bad! Pretty amazing resume. I've yet to come across such a resume on my desk at Jesus Image.

Even with such a past and pedigree, Solomon failed. He literally introduced idol worship to Israel. This is one of the most detestable sins. He married foreign wives and defiled the land. His family and Israel suffered greatly because of his prideful mixture of sin. Here is my question: Should we forever erase the very memory of Solomon from Scripture and all of his contributions to the eternal Kingdom of Jesus?

What is it in us that keeps from doing this? Why didn't God take him out and just kill him and diminish his impact? One of the reasons is the fact that he wore the oil. The anointing oil. The presence and power of the Holy Spirit.

The oil of the Spirit attracts the mercy, love, and grace of the Lord. It literally protects us from the wrath of God.

CLOSE TO HOME

Many of you know that my family is often in the public eye. The scrutiny has been intense over the years. More so for my wife than myself. Her entire childhood was full of the public's opinion finding its way into her life and family. Whether it was merited or not is not the point. Any time children are involved, it's painful. It is public knowledge that in 2010, my in-laws went through a divorce. The news traveled around the world so quickly. I'll never forget sitting in a hotel room with Jessica when the phone rang. It was a media outlet asking us questions about the scenario. I remember the pain and embarrassment that came. One moment, you're walking through packed stadiums being celebrated and thanked. The next moment, you're a liability. I still remember the pain of those with whom we were close disconnecting from us. I remember one leader saying, "Michael, your connection with your in-laws is an issue. Sorry, you're a liability." Doors began to close left and right for our then young ministry, Jesus Image. In preparation for an appearance on a television show, I was explicitly told,

"Don't mention your in-laws at all." Jessica and I were punished for decisions we never made. It was so tough to swallow. Although my immediate family had done nothing wrong, we were feeling the repercussions of the situation.

I remember being invited to a major university to preach at an on-campus ministry meeting. This was right in the thick of the divorce. Because I have a different last name than my wife's side of the family, they didn't place the connection. I was invited up to preach the Gospel to a large group of young people. Gainesville is about two hours from my house. Just before we jumped in the car to head up to the service, my phone rang.

"Hello," I said.

The caller replied, "Is this Michael?"

"This is Michael," I responded.

I'll never forget his question. He said, "Michael, what will you preach tonight?"

Well, whenever you hear something like that, you know something is up. Any time you answer that question with "Jesus," it's hard to argue. "I'll call you right back," the young man said. "How odd is that?" I thought to myself. Sure enough, he called back. I knew what was coming but just waited to see if I was right. He asked me, "Michael, are you Benny Hinn's son-in-law?" Without hesitation, I replied, "Yes, I am." His answer was sad and comical. "That's a real problem. That's a problem."

"Really?" I replied.

"Yes, it is a problem," he said.

I answered, "Is Benny preaching tonight? I love my father-in-law, but he won't be there. What's the issue? I'm preaching Jesus. What did I do?"

Incredibly flustered, he said, "Ahh…let me call you back again."

"No problem. But let me know what's going on because I am about to drive two hours and I need to know if you still want me to preach or not before I jump in the car with my family and friends."

He called back and said, "Fine, just come up. I guess we will let you speak, but we don't allow the gifts of the Spirit to operate."

I replied, "Fine, I'll come. I'm not coming to preach 'gifts.' I'm coming to preach Jesus." Little did this young man know how the Kingdom works. When the Gift Giver is preached and I yield to the Spirit, it's already too late. The Holy Spirit will pour His gifts into the thirsty and the open. My job was simply to minister to Jesus until those people became hungry.

The service was great, and Jesus was glorified. Afterward, I was swamped with young people thanking me. On my way out, that young leader walked up to me in tears. He cried, "I'm sorry, brother. I'm sorry. I judged you. You are a Christian!" It was quite moving and big of him to repent. I remember thinking, "Did you judge me so harshly that you didn't even think I was born again because of my familial affiliation?"

The depths we sink to when we begin to judge others is staggering. It kills the move of the Holy Spirit in ourselves and in our ministries. That group once had almost one thousand kids per Bible study. It shook America. Now it has dwindled to around one hundred attendees. I love them, but to be honest, some people there had the look of a funeral attendee rather than someone who had come to meet with God.

HONOR

Now, as you read this, is the Holy Spirit convicting you? Is He challenging you to honor those who have touched your life even if it costs you something? Who led you to Jesus? Have you spoken to that person lately? Did God use someone to bring physical healing to your body? Do you stay in touch with him or her? Perhaps God used someone who is controversial to bring an element of His presence into your life and change you forever. Do you speak kindly about that person? How about your parents, as imperfect as they may be? You wouldn't be here without them.

I personally believe that we should financially bless those who have impacted us spiritually. That includes our parents. Listen to the words of Paul the apostle: *"If we have sown spiritual things for you, is it a great thing if we reap your material things?"* (1 Cor. 9:11).

Heidi Baker says, "Love has to look like something." How true that is! Imagine if the Father said, "I love you" but had never sent Jesus. God's love is true and proven. The same is true regarding honor. It has to look like something. It has to cost us something.

Honor is huge to the Holy Spirit, regardless of the cost. During my in-laws' divorce, a pastor told me, "Michael, you should take Benny out of *The Jesus Book*. It could hurt the book. This is a pure book." I thought to myself, "Let's see…Benny was used by the Holy Spirit to:

- lead me to Jesus,
- lead me into the baptism of the Holy Spirit,
- bring healing to my body,
- teach me the Scriptures,
- teach me the beauty of worship,
- teach me the importance of the secret place,
- ordain me into the ministry,
- and to give me his daughter to marry!

"You take all that out and there is no Michael Koulianos. There is most definitely no Jesus Image or *Jesus Book*, for that matter. If that's what the cost is to be what many call 'successful' in ministry, I'm just not interested. We don't run away from those we love when they go through a difficult time. Our calling is to honor and to remain pure at the same time."

Maybe you're asking, "What does this have to do with the Holy Spirit?" The answer is a ton! When you honor what is of Him in the lives of people, you honor Him. I'm often asked, "To what do you attribute God's blessing and breakthrough in your life?" Here are a few answers:

- the love of Jesus
- time with Him
- prioritizing family
- honoring those who have been used by the Holy Spirit in my life

When we honor the Holy Spirit, He entrusts us with more of His presence. Why don't you ask the Lord today if you are properly honoring those who have been a blessing to you? If not, you can begin today!

Chapter Sixteen

TOUCH

In 2016, I was privileged to speak to hundreds of students in Pasadena, California. As I flew from California to Orlando, I began to think about God's calling on my life. There's no doubt that the Lord has entrusted me with the message of Jesus. I understand the weight and responsibility of stewarding a message that Heaven loves. I also know that sacred message has come directly from the heart of the Father through Jesus by the Spirit to my heart. But Jesus must be more to us than a topic, a historical figure, or a name on the pages of our Bible. He has to be more than the title of a sermon that we preach. As I began to contemplate my assignment, I realized that it was very simple: to preach Jesus and to lead people to a genuine encounter with the reality of His presence. The reality of His presence on earth is the Holy Spirit. I believe in my heart that I am nothing more than a follower of Jesus who leads people into a great and loving collision with the person of Jesus Himself.

I must say, it deeply saddens me when I hear leaders say that it doesn't matter what you feel and that we don't need God to touch us, we only need to believe the Bible. The problem with that thought process is that it is through the Bible that God wants to touch us. Did you know that the Bible is not about the Bible? Did you know that Scriptures are not about Scriptures? Did you know that church is not about the Bible? Did you know that God did not so love the world that He sent a Bible? You're probably experiencing a bit of a shock right now as you read this, but before you cast your opinion, let me say that the Bible is the inspired Word of God. The Bible is the heartbeat of God on paper. The Scriptures are alive. The Scriptures are the revealed will of God, and the living Scriptures plus the presence of the Spirit equal a revelation of Jesus, who is the face of the Father.

I would say I read my Bible as much or more than anyone I know. I love the Scriptures, and I love my physical copy of the Bible. It's been with me for years, and I've cried while reading it. To me, the Bible is much more than a book. It's an experience. Did you know that the church fathers called the Holy Scriptures "the book of experience"? But they were after something more. They were after the Person of the Bible. God did not give us the Bible to bring us back to the Bible. He gave us the Bible to bring us to Himself. And so, the Scriptures should lead us to the One who wrote them. After all, they do reveal His heart and His mind to us. Let me remind you, the Bible did not die on a cross, descend into hell, and get raised from the dead. Jesus did. Again, the Scriptures are one hundred percent divine and true from Genesis to Revelation. I am only making the point that there are many who own and read their Bibles who do not believe that Jesus is the Son of God. The bottom line is this: God gave us the Holy Scriptures so that we would meet Him.

Have you ever met someone? Of course you have. Did you shake their hand? Did you hug them? Perhaps you're from my part of the world, the eastern Mediterranean. Did you kiss them on both cheeks? How about when you got closer with them? Were hugs more consistent?

Let me ask you, when you met your spouse, did you just speak to them from a distance forever? Were you content with chatting on a computer or sending text messages from across the country? Did you marry them before you met them? Of course not. Genuine relationships require proximity, conversation, and yes, even touch. How much more does our loving Bridegroom, by the Holy Spirit, long to touch us? God wants you to feel His presence. God wants to touch you, and He wants you to touch Him back. You might say, "I'm not qualified to minister to the Lord or to touch Him." Was Thomas qualified while he doubted that Jesus had been raised from the dead? How did the Lord deal with him? He showed Thomas Himself—showed him His sounds and, ultimately, the feel of His holy body. The Holy Spirit wants to touch you.

I grew up in a realm of presence that I have yet to see today. I have stood on some of the world's greatest platforms. Some of the world's greatest churches and ministries have allowed me to minister. I've sat in on the meetings of incredible men and women. But I have yet to feel and experience the touch of the Holy Spirit like I did as a boy. It was like growing up in a greenhouse of glory. My heart would race at the opening song. I'd sprint into the church just to find a seat. I'd read my Bible with tears flowing, highlighting every single verse in front of me. I shook under the power of God so many times. I'd feel the wind blow over me in those days at the Orlando Christian Center. I remember the worship lifting to such a level that it felt like we had been taken straight to Heaven. I've been set on fire. I've been chilled with living water. I've felt the river of God flow in me, around me, and through me. I've felt tangible wind. I've felt the air vibrate and the ground under me shake while preaching. I've seen more than I ever thought I would, and I've been touched by the actual person of the Lord. My literal body, and heart, and mind have collided with the literal person of the Spirit.

If there is anything I would want you to experience and understand while reading this book, it would be this: how literal and real the person of the Holy Spirit is. No, He's not a concept. He's a real person. When you met your husband or your wife, you longed to get closer with time. He wants the same. He's not interested in a long-distance relationship that is merely full of lifeless information or historical facts regarding theology. He wants to touch you. Just as husband and wife kiss in the marriage ceremony, so the Lord is looking to get face to face with you and kiss you. *"Let him kiss me with the kisses of his mouth..."* (Song of Sol. 1:2). This shows the posture of heart that we should all have. We want God to kiss us. We don't want just one kiss; we want kisses. What does it take to be kissed by God? Well, it means to be face to face with Him. It means to stare into His eyes of fire—and that fire is the Holy Spirit Himself. Jesus has eyes of fire because He's full of the Spirit. And as we look into those eyes, we become Spirit and truth as His wonderful fire cleanses us and fills us with His love. We are mouth to mouth, where there is a literal breath exchange. Adam breathed in the Lord's breath, and we do the same as we look at Jesus and worship Him. This is impossible from far away, and it is equally impossible without touch.

Jesus knew the touch of God. Do you remember what happened while Jesus was on His way to raise that dead girl, the daughter of Jairus? As He was walking through the village, a woman with the issue of blood, weak and broken, crawled through the crowd just to get to Jesus. She had spent all her money on doctors. She was looked at by the entire community as being unclean. This poor woman, who some think was named Lydia, could not worship with the rest of her community or leave her home. She was rejected by society and completely broken, and her only hope came walking down the street. When she got to Jesus, she touched Him. Instantly, Jesus stopped in His tracks. He said, "Who touched Me?"

A disciple said, "Lord, what do You mean who touched You? Every-one's touching You."

He said, "No, someone touched Me. I felt power leave Me. I felt virtue leave Me." And He looked down and saw that woman, and she was healed (see Luke 8:43-48). Jesus was so sensitive to the activity of the Holy Spirit in His life that He could literally feel the power of God leave Him. Life in the Spirit is incredibly touch oriented. Have you ever asked yourself why God would give you such a beautiful spirit, soul, and body that is full of sensory receptors if He did not want you to be sensitive to Him?

Listen to the words of Micah the prophet: *"But truly I am full of power by the Spirit of the Lord..."* (Micah 3:8). Jeremiah said, "I have fire shut up in my bones" (see Jer. 20:9). When Daniel was touched by the Holy Spirit, He could hear his bones shaking (see Dan. 10:11). David said in Psalm 23:5: *"...my cup runneth over"* (KJV). All these verses have a very specific and clear language of relationship and intimacy. It is impossible to have intimacy with God and not hear Him, sense Him, see what He's doing, and feel His touch. Imagine if you wanted intimacy with your spouse but never wanted communication or touch.

I'm often asked, "Michael, how can I walk in the Spirit so that I can love Jesus?" What do you do when you pray? Tell me what your quiet time looks like. "I want to be closer with God." Well, I can't tell you exactly how you should commune with the Lord. I can offer you in the simplest way possible a description of how I spend time with God. Again, we all have our own walk with the Lord, and He deals differently with each of us. Yet the Scriptures do tell us that there are general and beautiful ways by which we all can enjoy His presence.

It's usually early in the morning before the sun is up. Before I open my eyes, I feel a pull deep within my heart. The pull is constant, strong, but not overly aggressive. It's heavy, but not burdensome. It seems to have hooks deep within my heart. Those hooks are attached to cords, as described in the following Scripture: "He draws me with cords of love" (see Hos. 11:4). This pull has a voice. The voice is very loving, and it's simple too. It says, "Michael, I'm here. Get up; I want to be with you. It's time to spend time together." Usually, a few minutes goes by until I can muster the strength to get up out of my bed, but I notice that before I'm fully awake, He's already tugging. So, I sit up and roll out of the bed as quietly as possible so that I don't wake up my wife. I grab a quick coffee to wake up, and I head to my prayer room. Jesus said in Matthew chapter 6, "When you pray, close the door," and so I simply obey (see Matt. 6:6). I close the door, grab my Bible, and usually just take a seat.

Before I begin to speak or say anything, I simply sit there. You say, "What do you do when you sit there?" Nothing… I take a deep breath, clear my mind. There are mornings where I'll whisper words of love and adoration to the Lord. It might sound something like this: "Jesus, You're beautiful. You're awesome. You're loving. You're kind. I love You. Thank You for waking me up this morning. Here I am. I worship You." And then, I wait some more. Why am I waiting? I'm not necessarily waiting for God to come, but I am waiting in His presence to be quickened by Him. You see, Saint Augustine said that he spent years looking for God *without,* while the entire time God was *within.* As I become still and release the cares of the world and just do nothing because I am fully dependent on Him, I will eventually sense the quickening of the Holy Spirit. Sometimes I physically feel it on my body. Sometimes I sense an instant connection with the activity of the Spirit. Sometimes He becomes very real and faith is born. Regardless, I do nothing until He quickens me. It's in that moment that I begin to praise Him.

David said, *"Be still, and know that I am God…"* (Ps. 46:10). The knowledge of God comes in this deep stillness as we wait upon the Lord. Knowledge of God means to know God, not to know about Him. It's in this place of waiting upon Him that you discover His person, His qualities, His likes, and His dislikes. So, I wait. How long? It just depends. I'm not waiting on the clock. I am waiting on the Person.

Once I feel that quickening, I then begin to open my mouth and praise the Lord. I give Him glory because He's amazing. I might say something like, "Jesus, You're God Almighty. You've been crucified and raised, and you're seated on the throne. You are the Victorious One. You've defeated death. You're amazing." Sometimes I'll go through His works and His acts in the Scriptures, and when I begin to praise the Lord, I'll sense the reality of His Kingdom in the moment. What do I mean by that? His presence—the presence of the Spirit—begins to rule over me. It overshadows my senses. It overshadows my weakness. It overshadows my fallen desires. And the Kingdom that is within me begins to rule and reign. From then on, I just follow His lead. I've learned to let the Holy Spirit be my teacher in my quiet time. He might say, "Open your Bible." He might say, "Wait again." He might say, "Sing to Me in the Spirit. Sing to Me an old hymn." Whatever He says, I lovingly obey. I've found that it's in that moment that my desires become one with His. So, what I desire, I simply yield to. If I desire to read the Scriptures, I follow that. If I desire to do nothing, I follow that.

There comes a time, when I'm with the Lord, when every desire but a desire for Him dies. That can usually take a while. Once I get to the place where I have one desire, and that is Jesus, I know I'm entering a deep place in the Holy Spirit. It is in this place that your body literally cries out for the presence of God to fill and touch it.

Let's have a look at the great man of prayer, King David.

O God, You are my God; I shall seek You earnestly; my soul thirsts for You, my flesh yearns for You, in a dry and weary land where there is no water. Thus I have seen You in the sanctuary, to see Your power and Your glory. Because Your lovingkindness is better than life, my lips will praise You. So I will bless You as long as I live; I will lift up my hands in Your name. My soul is satisfied as with marrow and fatness, and my mouth offers praises with joyful lips. When I remember You on my bed, I meditate on You in the night watches, for You have been my help, and in the shadow of Your wings I sing for joy. My soul clings to You; Your right hand upholds me. But those who seek my life to destroy it, will go into the depths of the earth. They will be delivered over to the power of the sword; they will be a prey for foxes. But the king will rejoice in God; everyone who swears by Him will glory, For the mouths of those who speak lies will be stopped (Psalm 63:1-11 NASB).

Notice David says in verse 1: *"…my flesh longeth for Thee in a dry and thirsty land, where no water is"* (Ps. 63:1 KJV). I do not believe that we are called to live in dryness. Jesus paid a price for our continual fellowship with the Lord. If we ever do suffer distance from the Lord, it's never the Lord's fault. But David here wanted more, and he came to the place where he wanted his body to experience the life-giving water of the Spirit.

It's in these times of prayer that I feel completely overwhelmed with His presence. But the language does not become complicated; in fact, it becomes simpler. In that moment, I am not a preacher. I am not an evangelist. I am simply a child of God. And so, my language becomes more singular, more childlike, more basic. You might hear something like this: "Jesus, I love You. Jesus, I need You. You are beautiful." Or you might hear, "Holy Spirit, fill me." Sometimes my heart cries, "I just want You." Then I wait some more and enjoy His beautiful presence. It seems to come like wave after wave after wave. There are spikes, there are peaks, and there are valleys. And so, in the valleys, I wait for Him to sweep through again. In the peaks, I enjoy Him. Once He quickens me, I can share intimate, loving language that ministers back to Him. At the end of the day, I want Him to smile.

Even our prayer time ends with His joy. He receives joy when we receive His joy, but in my heart I want Him to be full of joy when our time is through. You might ask, "When do you stop?" The Scriptures explain this beautifully. In Song of Solomon 8:4, the Bible says, "...*Do not stir up nor awaken love until it pleases.*" I wait until the Lord is through with me, and when I feel that release, I am done. I must say as a comical side note, He's yet to kick me out of the secret place because He's through with me. If I were to spend three hours there, it would seem like He wanted four. If I were to spend eight, it would seem like He wanted nine. If I were to spend my entire day, it would seem like He wanted another. That is how He keeps us coming.

Chapter Seventeen

WHEN HE COMES

*A*nd John bore witness saying, 'I saw the Spirit descending from heaven like a dove, and He remained upon Him'" (John 1:32). Yes, Jesus was the Son of God. There is absolutely no doubt about that. But even He waited on the Holy Ghost to descend on Him before beginning any ministry. Here's a question we all need to ask ourselves, whether we are Evangelicals, Pentecostals, Charismatics, Baptists, Methodists, Catholics, or Orthodox Christians: If Jesus did not think that the coming of the Spirit upon Him and us was so necessary, why would He wait thirty years to do anything until the Holy Spirit actually came upon Him tangibly? If anyone could've depended on knowledge, experience, and wisdom to follow God, it was Jesus.

Certainly, He has a pretty amazing resume. I mean, after all, according to John 1, He is the creator of everything. The Bible says, *"All things were made by Him; and without Him was not any thing made that was made"* (John 1:3 KJV). We know that Jesus is eternal. The Scripture John 1:1 says, *"In the beginning was the Word, and the Word was with*

God…." He is all consuming, and everything lives in Him. Colossians 1 says, *"…in Him all things consist"* (Col. 1:17). On top of that, He holds all things together. Hebrews tells us, "He holds all things together by the word of His power" (see Heb. 1:3).

He is a lion, and He is a lamb. He suffered; died; went into the earth; conquered death, hell, and the grave; and made an open show and embarrassing display of the devil. After He got through annihilating hell and every demon, on the third day He broke through the earth like a mighty warrior, cracked open the tomb, folded His grave clothes, and walked out as *"the firstborn among many brethren"* (Rom. 8:29). Jesus was the captain of the Lord's hosts as He introduced Himself to Joshua (see Josh. 5:14). Jesus is perfectly portrayed in Exodus 12 as the lamb whose blood was smeared on the two doorposts and the lintel by the children of Israel (see Exod. 12:7,23). Jesus was there standing on the rock in front of Gideon (see Judg. 6:21). It was Jesus who came and appeared to Abraham with two angels, discussing His judgment that would come upon Sodom and Gomorrah (see Gen. 18:16-33). When the Lord covered Adam and Eve with animal skins, He was telling the world about His Son, Jesus—that one day He would come to shed His blood to pay for our sin (see Gen. 3:21). The ark is not so much about a boat and water; rather, it is a picture of Jesus, the Ark who keeps us safe from the judgments of the world. The window of the ark is not about a window or a window treatment (see Gen. 6:16); rather, it speaks of the side of Jesus being opened and the Holy Spirit being released upon His death as water and blood poured out.

The entire Bible is about Jesus. The Lord even said that in John chapter 5. He said, "The Scriptures speak of Me" (see John 5:39). So, my friend, I think it's safe to say that Jesus has a pretty amazing resume and is qualified to be in the ministry, but even Jesus refused to do anything on His own without the presence and power of the Holy Spirit on His life. So how much more should we depend on the Spirit! Why don't you ask the Lord now to overwhelm you with His precious presence? Because the impossible in your life becomes possible in a moment as you open up to the Holy Spirit.

DEPENDENCY

Even after Jesus conquered death victoriously and set us free for eternity, the Bible says in Acts 1 that *"…He through the Holy Spirit had given commandments to the apostles whom He had chosen"* (Acts 1:2). Do you see four incredible words in that verse? *Through the Holy Spirit.*

Let me attempt to give you a picture of what was taking place. Jesus has been raised from the dead as the first fruits, as a new breed—literally, a new race that the earth had never seen. There He was, with wounds in His hands, feet, and side, in a glorious resurrected state, sitting with His disciples. They decided to have a Bible study. Can you imagine having a Bible study with the glorified Son of God? But Jesus refused to have even a mere Bible study unless it was through the Holy Spirit. We have to understand that it is only through the Holy Spirit that we have any connection to the Lord and any ability to reveal Him to others.

So, if the perfect resurrected and victorious Christ depended on the Spirit, my question to you is simply this: How much more do we, as frail humans, need the Spirit in our lives? You see, the presence and power of the Spirit trumps every method and plan. And He will take every weakness and hole in our lives and fill it with His presence. That is why the Bible says, *"Let the weak say, 'I am strong'"* (Joel 3:10). It is not a sin to be weak. In fact, our weakness, once handed to the Lord, becomes a mighty force to be reckoned with. He takes those who are not qualified and qualifies them with the anointing of the Spirit. And so, today He looks around and searches the world through and through, not for perfect people, but for people who know they need Him.

As I've indicated before, my favorite preacher in history is Kathryn Kuhlman. As I watch video recordings of her ministering, I'm blown away by the tenderness with which she ministers and the dependence that she has on the Holy Spirit. I can hear her words today: "Please don't grieve Him. Don't grieve the Holy Spirit. He is all I've got." That's dependency, and that's why God chose to use her. God is drawn to people who do not believe that they are capable to do His work with their own ability, and nobody exemplified that quality more than Kathryn Kuhlman. She was convinced of her inability, and because of that, she yielded to God's ability. One of my favorite quotes from Miss Kuhlman is this: "He doesn't choose golden vessels. He doesn't choose silver vessels. He chooses willing vessels."

You know, I didn't write this book to be an instruction manual. My prayer is that all who read it will literally meet the Holy Spirit. But why don't you say this to the Lord right now:

Jesus, I'm hungry for You, I need Your presence. Holy Spirit, You are the presence of Jesus. I am not qualified to change the world in my own strength, but if You touch me, I can. I want to know You with everything in me. I want to meet You. I want to be Your friend.

He is beautiful. I've met so many who have shied away from the ways of the Holy Spirit because of fear. They become nervous because of things they've seen or heard regarding life in the Spirit. Some of the examples they cite are actually the work of the Holy Spirit, some are not, but it would be foolish to throw out all the Holy Spirit is simply because a few have mishandled Him.

The Holy Spirit is not owned by Pentecostals or Charismatics. In fact, He is a person whom we receive but do not own. How can a human own God? I want to say clearly that no denomination has exclusive rights to the person of the Holy Spirit. All Christians have the

Holy Spirit living on the inside of them. Jesus breathed on His disciples and said, *"Receive the Holy Spirit"* (John 20:22). This was the moment of their conversion. I've met Orthodox priests, Lutheran pastors, Baptist ministers, and Catholic priests who have all been walking in a flourishing, vibrant, and powerful relationship with the Holy Spirit.

In fact, I just preached in a Catholic conference in Toulon, France, that was led by a Catholic priest named Jean-Michel. The tent in which it was held was the former tent of John II. There were nuns and priests sitting in the crowd. A priest even got healed as I began to worship the Lord and minister to the sick. These Catholics were glowing with the Holy Spirit.

It might surprise you to know that before the Charismatic Renewal there were no Charismatics by name. The Charismatic movement did not start with Charismatics; it started with two hungry priests crying out to the Lord for a miracle. On top of that, the pope prayed for a second Pentecost in the Catholic Church, and the Holy Spirit was released. That outpouring that happened initially in Indiana with the Catholics spread to the Assemblies of God and filtered into all denominations and shook the world, and we are still riding that wave today. The point is this: The Holy Spirit is not intimidated by our boundaries, yet He will never force Himself on our lives. He does not look at me as a former Orthodox. He just knows me as Michael.

I encourage you get to know the Holy Spirit for yourself. Don't let how others have treated Him cause you to reject Him. Regardless of what some have made the experience of walking with the Holy Spirit, use Jesus' life alone as your example and you will find that the Holy Spirit is beautiful, tender, powerful, and sacred. Besides the countless miracles that Jesus performed, did you know that it was the Holy Spirit who raised Jesus from the dead? *"And He was shown to be the Son of God when He was raised from the dead by the power of the Holy Spirit. He is Jesus Christ our Lord"* (Rom. 1:4 NLT). There would have been no resurrection without the Holy Spirit. So don't worry about what you've seen or heard; just look at Him. Look at Jesus as your example. Look straight into His eyes of fire. Why are His eyes afire? Because the Holy Spirit is fire within Him and around Him. As you look to Jesus regarding the Holy Spirit, all of your fear will disappear. You can trust Him today.

I can remember telling others and myself that I will never act in certain ways even if the power of God touches me. My framework was broader than most, but now, after years of getting to know the Lord, I have found that I was incredibly narrow-minded. I was okay with people being saved, healed, filled with the Holy Spirit, prophesying, speaking in tongues, and, of course, falling down. I grew up around people being slain in the Holy Spirit, and that began happening in all of my meetings; but I said to myself, "That is I as far as I want to go. I'm not going any further." Well, God had many experiences up His sleeve just to prove to me that He is not the God of my box; He's the God of the universe. He's the infinite God who can do whatever He pleases, and if we give Him our lives, He may just shock us by how He touches us.

A friend of mine named Chris Klimis once said, "I learned when God filled me with His joy, the joy of the Spirit, that God was not interested first and foremost in how cool I looked when He touched me." Just look at David. The Holy Spirit comes upon Him as he celebrates the entry of the ark into Jerusalem, and he begins to dance uncontrollably. And his wife, the daughter of Saul, who was used to the old way, the old regime, ridiculed him (see 2 Sam. 6:14-16). And this happens today as we give our lives over to Him. We may just be a little more undignified than we are comfortable with, and very likely more undignified than others are comfortable with.

I attended a conference held by Randy Clark and Bill Johnson in Orlando in 2010. I will never forget the conference. A friend of mine got me great seats. I sat there as Randy ministered. I had never seen Randy in person before. Of course I had heard about how the Lord used him in the Toronto Blessing and how He had used him around the world to bring healing to so many thousands of lives. I had great honor and respect for Randy.

As I sat in the meeting, I noticed how he talked very calmly. In fact, I was blown away by how relaxed he was when he preached—yet the people in the room were sitting on the edge of their seats. And Randy, with his southern accent, just talked about God's will to heal, the different ways that the Lord brings healing, and the new levels of healing that he believed the Lord was bringing to the world in this season.

Bill Johnson was to my right. At that time, I had met Bill only a few times. Bill had always been a hero to me because of his desire to steward the presence of God. And so, sitting next to him was a real privilege and delight.

Halfway into Randy's sermon, he took a step toward the crowd from the pulpit. I would say he walked about five feet from the pulpit toward the crowd. Well, since I was in the front row, I was only about two feet away from him when he began to walk toward the crowd. Immediately, my hands starting shaking, I thought to myself, "Uh, is something wrong with me?" Randy then took a step backward toward the pulpit, and my hand stopped shaking. He stepped forward again, and then both hands started shaking. It's interesting and incredibly humorous to me that the Lord chose to manifest His power in my body in the form of shaking. The Bible says that Daniel shook to the degree that he heard his bones rattle (see Dan. 10:11). Well, my shaking wasn't as intense as that, but it was uncontrollable.

I used to say, when I pastored in Southern California, that I would never be one of those people who shook their hands when they prayed. I met many people from prayer movements in America and overseas who would shake their hands when they prayed. To be honest, I thought they were all crazy and in the flesh. Now here I was shaking uncontrollably in my hands and Bill and other respected teachers and preachers were sitting next to me. I thought to myself, "How stupid do I look? These guys are so calm and here I am unable to stop my hands from violently shaking." My only option was to try and hide my hands so I jammed them into my pockets. Well, now they were shaking inside my pants.

Finally, I said to myself, "What are You trying to show me, Lord?" Well, number one, the shaking told me much about the anointing on Randy and what he carried. It showed me that volume of preaching does not equate to power. It taught me that a genuine life given to God becomes a tangible glory-carrier to a generation. It also reminded me never to tell God how He can and cannot do things. So, just trust the Lord. Don't worry about how He touches you. Don't tell Him He can or cannot do His work in your life unless it's by your standard. He is a faithful Shepherd.

Chapter Eighteen

PRESENCE AND POWER

H ave you ever been in a meeting where power is flowing but there is no beauty in the air? No moisture on the words of the person who's speaking? The name of Jesus is not being exalted? Perhaps somebody's giving a prophetic word, sharing details about a person's life and past, but nothing in your heart burns. You don't long to spend more time with Jesus after you hear him or her speak. People may even be healed, but you have no desire to come back the next day. Have you ever asked yourself what brings people to us who are not sick and are born again? It's the presence of God. Oftentimes we don't understand the difference between God's power and God's presence. God's power sets the captives free. God's power destroys the works of the devil. God's presence helps me fellowship with the Lord.

PRESENCE

As I said earlier in this book, when Jesus breathed upon the disciples and said, *"Receive the Holy Spirit"* (John 20:22), the Holy Spirit began to live inside of them. In that moment, they became the temple of the Holy Ghost. No matter where they went or who they were with, they carried the presence of the Lord on the inside of them. This is what it means to be born again. As the glory of God lives in the Holy of Holies, in the tabernacle in the wilderness, our bodies have now become tabernacles for the Holy Spirit. This is a beautiful and holy gift, perhaps the greatest gift we could ever receive—the indwelling Spirit of God. This is the presence of God in our hearts. When the storms are raging around us, there is always peace within, and we are always able to retreat into that beautiful tabernacle that is our heart. And as Jesus said, Heaven is within us (see Luke 17:21). This is why Jesus calmed the storm as He slept during the storm. Yes, there was a storm around Him, but within Him there was perfect peace because His peace was not ruled by what went on around Him. He affected what went on around Him through the presence of God within Him. This is how we are to live.

Are you stressed? Do you have anxiety? Do you feel like the world around you controls you? This could be because you don't know how to find the Lord's presence. Or should I say it this way: You don't know *where* to find the Lord's presence. It is within you. What an advantage we have! We literally carry the Kingdom of God within us, who is the King Himself.

I have found that the beauty of the Lord is found in His presence. I remember attending a prophetic meeting in Los Angeles years ago. The man leading the meeting was a good man—very kind. I have great respect for him. He began to give names and details of people's lives, but something in me did not yearn to come back the following night. I thought to myself, "I am seeing amazing things. Why don't I want to come back?" It's because there was a gift in operation. Now, if a gift is manifesting more predominantly than presence, then I will draw people to my gift instead of the presence. Remember, the power of God upon us sets people free around us. The presence of God within us is the key to my personal fellowship with the Lord.

Let's remember a truth and never forget it: The power flows from the presence of God. The presence of God does not find its origin in the power of God. The power of God flows from Him, and He is the presence. Habakkuk says it this way:

Lord, I have heard the report about You and I fear. O Lord, revive Your work in the midst of the years, in the midst of the years make it known; in wrath remember mercy. God comes from Teman, and the Holy One from Mount Paran. Selah. His splendor covers the heavens, And the earth is full of His praise. His radiance is like the sunlight; He has rays flashing from His hand, and there is the hiding of His power (Habakkuk 3:2-4 NASB).

The hiding of His power comes from His person. It comes from Him. *"His radiance is like the sunlight,"* verse 4 says. *"He has rays flashing from His hand, and there is the hiding of His power."* His hand is Jesus always. The hand of the Lord in the Old Testament speaks of Jesus Himself. So many people want power, yet they've never gone to the Lord of power and discovered Him. Let's remember that the presence of the Lord is the Lord Himself. So, when the Lord breathed on those disciples, they received His indwelling presence. This was enough for them to go to Heaven and fellowship with Him every day at any moment. Today, if you know Jesus, you carry the presence of the Lord. He has promised to never leave us or forsake us, even until the end of the age (see Heb. 13:5).

POWER

Acts 1:8 says, *"Ye shall receive power, after that the Holy Ghost is come upon you..."* (KJV). Remember that Jesus is speaking to the same disciples that He spoke to when He breathed on them and said, *"Receive the Holy Spirit"* (John 20:22). Why would He tell them to wait for power if they already had power? It's because they had not been entrusted with the power of the Holy Spirit yet. They had been entrusted with the indwelling presence of the Spirit. This was a different experience of which the Lord was speaking. Since they had already been filled internally, He now wanted to clothe them externally. He wanted to change their nature and even their personalities, and make their weaknesses strengths so that the world would meet Jesus. Jesus is clear here that if we wait, we shall receive power. There is no ifs, ands, or buts connected to this promise: "Wait and you shall receive." Who are we waiting on? Or what are we waiting on? Jesus said that the coming of the Holy Spirit upon us was the promise of the Father (see Luke 24:49). If the Father promises something, you can bet your bottom dollar that He wants to give it to you. The key is waiting on the Lord, who is the baptizer. Jesus said that He would pray to the Father and that the Father would send the Holy Spirit (see John 14:16).

Now, just think of this for a moment. Let's look at the words of Jesus. John 14:16 says, *"And I will pray the Father, and He shall give you another Comforter, that He may abide with you for ever"* (KJV). Isn't this beautiful? Let's look at this simple spiritual equation for a moment. The coming of the Holy Spirit upon you is the promise of the Father. You have Jesus praying to the Father for you to receive the power of the Holy Spirit. When Jesus prays, the Father does it. *That* I can assure you, my friend. Perhaps you've thought for a long time, "Well, maybe I just don't qualify for the power of God. Maybe I have too much sin in my life. Maybe I've messed up too much in the past." Did you know that your past means nothing to the Lord once you come to Jesus and ask Him to forgive your sin? There is not a single one of us alive today who earns the power of the Holy Spirit outside of the mercy and grace of the blood of Jesus. We have qualified for the power of the Holy

Spirit because Jesus has qualified us through His sinless life, death, burial, resurrection, and ascension. It is His work that we are grafted into, receiving blessings that we don't deserve! Many believe that they have to be good enough to receive the power of the Holy Spirit, but they never realize that it's the power of the Holy Spirit that changes them in a much profounder way than all their efforts in the natural combined. It's very important you realize that God wants you to walk in His power for a reason—so that others will meet Jesus. The next time you doubt God's desire to give you the power of the Holy Spirit, remember the promise of Jesus: *"Ye shall receive power"* (Acts 1:8 KJV).

WHAT'S THE TRUE SIGN OF THE HOLY SPIRIT BAPTISM?

Many believe that certain gifts must manifest when somebody has had a legitimate Holy Spirit baptism. That is not my perspective, but I respect the others who believe this way. The true evidence that some-body has been empowered by the Holy Spirit is not the gift of tongues, according to Jesus. For Him, the true sign is power. Power to do what? To be a witness unto Jesus to the ends of the earth. Notice Jesus did not say that we will witness once we have received the power of the Holy Spirit. He said we will be a witness (see Acts 1:8). Your life liter-ally becomes a testimony of who Jesus is to the entire world around you once the Holy Spirit plugs you into power from Heaven. That power dethrones and destroys the influence of the devil in people's lives.

Acts 10:38 says, *"God anointed Jesus of Nazareth with the Holy Spirit and power, and how He went around doing good and healing all who were under the power of the devil, because God was with Him"* (NIV). How do we know if somebody has received the power of the Holy Spirit? Well, it's quite simple. We go around doing good, healing flows through our lives, physical and mental illnesses are healed, inner healing is available, and the power of the devil is destroyed. Why? Because God is with us. The power of the Holy Spirit sets people free. It is literally the ammunition of Heaven against what binds millions of people around you today. I want to be very clear about this: Without the power of the Holy Spirit, people stay unsaved, they stay sick, they stay depressed, and fear will continue to dominate them. Sickness mocks all of us unless we are clothed with the power of the Holy Spirit. It is not a side issue. It is not a minor benefit on top of a ministry that we create. Unless our lives are flowing in the power of the Holy Spirit, we don't have a ministry.

Remember Zechariah 4:6: "'It is not by might, it is not by power, but it is by My Spirit,' says the Lord" (see Zech. 4:6). The moment we realize that no matter how smart and organized we feel we are, while it might look in the natural like things are happening, nothing eternal takes place outside of the power of the Holy Spirit. If Jesus needed the power of the Holy Spirit, we need it today. It's important to remember, however, that this is not a vague power. It is not a higher power. It is a power that flows from a person; that's why it's called the power of the Holy Spirit. This power enforces the heart of the person.

Let me explain. The heart of God, the Holy Spirit, is to glorify Jesus. Jesus is glorified when He receives what He paid for. For example, Jesus paid for the salvation of the entire world. Every time somebody is genuinely saved, it glorifies Jesus. It says to the princes and the principalities of the air, to Heaven, and to everybody standing around on the earth that Jesus is enough to change our lives, that He is alive, and that He is still King over our sin. Every time somebody is healed, it glorifies Jesus because it brings into the here and now what the Scripture says Jesus paid for: "...*by His stripes we are healed*" (Isa. 53:5). It shows that God is faithful to His promises. When a demon is cast out, it says that God has come. As Jesus said, "When devils are cast out, it's because the Kingdom has come" (see Luke 11:20; Matt. 12:28). It reveals to the world that Jesus is greater than any power in the universe.

So, the power of the Spirit fights for the heartbeat of God. It fights and declares and installs the will of God. When darkness tries to stop what God intends and has paid for, the power of God is needed. Bill Johnson puts it this way: "Our authority is like the policeman's badge, but our power is like the policeman's gun. The power is needed to enforce what the badge stands for." The power of the Holy Spirit enforces what our authority stands for, which is Jesus Himself.

Now, have you ever met people who seem to have power but live like the devil? Have you ever wondered how could God use them—*why* God would use them? It's quite simple. While they neglect the presence, the power still remains. The Scripture says, *"The gifts and calling of God are without repentance"* (Rom. 11:29 KJV). In other words, they are not taken away. This power brings giftings along with it. While the presence of God is in them—the Bible says there's an anointing that dwells within us that we don't need anyone to teach us (see 1 John 2:27)—this is this internal presence. While they may be neglecting the presence of God within, the power of God upon them still remains. Why is this? It's not so much for them as it is for those with whom they come in contact.

Do you remember the parable that says that tares found their way into the harvest field? The landowner said, "Let us wait until the harvest until we remove the tares because it might ruin the harvest. Once the harvest comes, the tares will be thrown into the fire" (see Matt. 13:29-30). Oftentimes the Lord will allow somebody who's living in sin to continue to flow in power for the sake of the people who are being set free by the power. Elijah was fed meat by ravens during the drought and famine in the wilderness (see 1 Kings 17:6). Ravens were a cursed bird, but God was interested in Elijah. He was willing to feed Elijah through an animal that was cursed. This is a truth we must remember: Just because God is setting others free through our lives, it does not mean that we are free.

Chapter Nineteen

THE SECRET OF MIRACLES

Jesus was on a mission to reveal the Father to the world. He was the literal embodiment and perfect image of the Father. Hebrews 1 tells us that Jesus is the very *"brightness of His glory"* (Heb. 1:3). Jesus is not only the brightness of God's glory; He is the very brightness of His glory. He is the top of the top. He is the apex of God's highest height. He is the brightest light and the crescendo of God. So, to look at Him is to see absolute holy perfection. He is the Word of God. The Bible says, *"The Word became flesh and dwelt among us..."* (John 1:14).

Do you remember when He said, *"Out of the abundance of the heart the mouth speaks"* (Matt. 12:34)? He was teaching us a powerful principle about how our words are the fruit of our hearts. In other words, to know someone's heart, just listen to his or her words for a while. What we say reveals what is within us. While this explains a great deal to us about our own lives and words, this beautiful principle also allows access into the character of God Himself. Remember, God created us in His image. This means that God's words flow from His heart too. To know His heart, we simply listen to His voice and read His Word. To know His heart, we must ask ourselves, "What is God speaking?" Or, to be more precise: *"Who* is God speaking? *Who* is God saying to you and me?"

The Bible also tells us in Hebrews 1, *"In these last days* [God has] *spoken to us by His Son…"* (Heb. 1:2) Another way to think of this is to say, "He has spoken His Son to us." So, what is the Father saying? It's really simple, my friend. He is always saying, "JESUS." It is His only message and sermon. Why is this? It's because of what Jesus told us. From the abundance of the Father's heart His mouth speaks. Where did Jesus come from? The Scriptures tells us clearly: He was *"in the bosom of the Father"* (John 1:18). Jesus literally is the heartbeat of our loving Father. To see Jesus is to see the heart of the Father. To receive Jesus is to receive the Father's heart and only sermon.

This is amazing for many reasons! It shows me that Jesus is my absolute perfect pattern and model. That means what He did, I must do. His life is my gauge. You know what? He didn't attempt to serve His Father by setting people free without the Holy Spirit. Jesus knew that without the Holy Spirit empowering His earthly ministry, His ministry would have been powerless. There would have been absolutely no healings. Signs and wonders would never have been witnessed by the thousands. The hungry would have remained hungry. The woman with the issue of blood would have eventually bled to death. The crippled would have died on their mats. Demons would have remained in the tormented. This may be hard for you to imagine, but we need to understand that without the Holy Spirit, Jesus' ministry would have been ineffective. Yes, the Holy Spirit is a person. But He is also the power of the Trinity.

WAIT FOR POWER FROM ON HIGH

Remember, if Jesus is our pattern and truth, He would never ask us to do something that He Himself did not do. Jesus told His disciples to "wait in Jerusalem until you are empowered from on high" (see Luke 24:49). He knows the feeling of waiting. He waited for the power of the Holy Spirit for thirty years. The disciples only waited for ten days. Why would He instruct us to wait for the Holy Spirit? Because without His power, we don't have a chance of revealing Jesus. With His power, revealing Jesus is natural and normal.

I've personally prayed for tens of thousands of sick people since 1989. I have seen more and greater miracles than I ever thought I would. Early on in my ministry, the Lord began to teach me something loud and clear: The devil doesn't recognize who I am friends with. He doesn't care if I'm part of a big church or a small church. He is not going to leave someone I am praying for because of the size of my social media following. Neither does he care if I have famous friends and family. This one may ruffle some feathers—but he doesn't care about the length of time I have been saved. Only two things are of issue when praying for the sick and oppressed: whose you are and who is on you. Let me make it plain and simple, and maybe a little old school: Is there Holy Ghost power flowing through your being? You see, my friend, you can't say, "In the name of my church, be healed." You can't say, "In the name of my favorite preacher, be healed." This is what matters: the name of Jesus in the power of the Holy Spirit. The enemy knows if you've been rocked by the Holy Spirit. He has a good eye for finding those who are clothed with the Spirit. Why? Because he's afraid of the One who clothes us. He runs from Him. He hates the Holy Spirit and His Power because he knows his slimy grip on people's lives is destroyed when he bumps into heavenly power. Remember what the Bible says: "It is the anointing that breaks the yoke" (see Isa. 10:27).

Chapter Twenty

STEWARDS OF THE HOLY SPIRIT

Journeying through these stories that you have just read throughout this book, I'm completely blown away by the grace of God. As I look back at my life and our ministry, it's impossible not to see the fingerprints of those who paid a dear price so that I could walk in a deeper measure of God. First of all, I owe the Lord everything, but I also owe His friends so much. There is an inheritance in the Holy Spirit. God's way in this area is always multiplication. It's His desire that we go from glory to glory. His government is always increasing. I truly believe that this generation is to walk in a greater measure of the Holy Spirit than the generation before us. When I think of the breakthrough in the lives of the champions of the generation before mine, I am blown away by the mark they have set. We have a lot of work to do, friends. Yet in the Lord, everything is possible. I believe a greater flow of the Holy Spirit is going to hit the world and the Church than we've ever seen in our lives. I believe the greatest outpouring of the Spirit is about to touch the earth. But as we step into this and seek God, let's never forget those who have touched our lives.

I'd like this to be a chapter full of honor. Maybe it would make me look more self-sufficient if I looked at you and said that everything I have experienced in the Lord came through a sovereign encounter while being alone with Him, but that's just not the case. If you trace church history, it's never been the case. I absolutely believe that God is looking for cooperation, for co-laborers on the earth. He wants to share His activity and desire with His friends. If you look back at your life, I'm sure you can trace every encounter with God to the cooperation of one of God's friends. That combination impacted you, and I pray that will be said of us in the years to come—that you and I were used to impact others in the Holy Spirit. So, I would like to honor some of the people who have deeply impacted me forever. There are many more of you who have touched my life than I have room to mention in this book. I am so grateful for all those who have paid a price so that I could know the Lord more deeply.

MY PARENTS

My parents, Theo and Evelyn Koulianos, are true Christians. They will be the first to tell you that they're not perfect, but their example of humility, loyalty, and faithfulness to God framed my view of Jesus forever. I can still remember coming home at night backslidden away from God and drunk. Some nights turned into mornings and I'd get home at 6:30 A.M. I'd walk through the door, and my mom would be there sitting on a rocking chair without having slept a wink, just praying, speaking in tongues over my life, declaring the works of God in my future, agreeing with prophetic destiny that was prophesied over me as a boy through my father-in-law. I'd come in staggering, and she'd be there rocking back and forth, praying in the Spirit, saying things like this: "He will stand before kings and queens. He will preach the Gospel to the nations. He will change the world for Jesus."

I remember one early morning when I came in—it was 1999; my mom had been up all night praying for me. There she was, praying and watching *This Is Your Day*. I walked in the house and felt the presence of God. I was so deeply convicted, so depressed because of where my life had gone. I knew that I was not yielding to my prophetic future. Instead, I was following the devil and my own ambitions. My heart was so empty. And there was my mom, never giving up, always declaring, always standing in the gap. Pastor Benny came on the screen, and my mom looked at me and said, "One day you'll be a preacher just like Pastor Benny, and not only will you be a preacher, one day you'll stand alongside him and preach the Gospel with him." You have to understand, I did not have a very close relationship with Pastor Benny at the time. He was living in California, and I was in college in Florida. I hadn't seen him in years, hadn't spoken to him in years. This kind of prophetic word seemed so outside the box, it sounded like it was crazy. To be honest, I thought my mom had gone crazy. Looking back, I was the crazy one for not believing. To think I've stood on platforms across the world and shared pulpits before thousands, preaching the Gospel and ministering to the sick with my father-in-law.

My parents are humble. They understand what it means to go low. They're the first ones there when something hits our family. They're a rock of support and a bridge of hope.

My dad has been through so many ups and downs. We went from having millions of dollars to losing it all when I was about twelve years old. I remember leaving our home because it was foreclosed on. I remember the Mercedes Benz being taken away and replaced with an old pickup truck. I remember my dad leaving the house at 5:30 in the morning to go work in the flea market after we lost everything, yet his faith stayed strong. Every night he came home, read his Bible, and talk about Jesus. Our home was full of joy, full of happiness, which was possible only because it was full of God. My parents were the gateway by which God could flood our home and lovingly distract us from the hardships we were facing. My dad was at every golf tournament and at most practices, coached my football team, and today he's still the first one to serve in our meetings, to pray for us, and to stand with us no matter what. My dad taught me to hold on to Jesus when everything else collapses.

My mom always had a meal on the table. Our clothes were always meticulous. Nothing was wrinkled. Our house was always spotless, and she was always praying while keeping it that way. She prayed so hard for me while I was away from God and so consistently that I actually memorized her tongues language. If she knew I had been out all night, she'd stand outside the door or go into the shower and pray loudly enough to make sure I could hear her. I recall lying in bed, tortured by her loud praying as she declared and prophesied over my future. I remember her pleading the blood of Jesus every day over my spirit, my soul, and my body. I remember those prophetic words of standing before kings, and priests, and great leaders of nations; the first time it happened, her prophetic words leapt in my spirit.

My parents have had the greatest influence on my life. Mom and Dad, thank you for loving Jesus, and thank you for loving me, Jessica, and the children.

BENNY HINN

As I'm sure you've found while reading this book, so much of what I've had the joy of experiencing in the Holy Spirit is due to the life of Benny Hinn. Never once did Benny teach me how to heal the sick. He never gave me three steps for miracles. What he did teach me as a young boy and as a young man was how to cherish the presence of the Holy Spirit.

When Jessica and I decided to date, he asked that I move into the house and be his personal assistant. It was the hardest job I've ever had, I promise you that. But I had the joy of watching him seek the Lord every morning, and I knew never to go near that room while he was alone with God. This began to forge in my own life a consistent daily contact with the Holy Spirit. I began to treasure the presence of God above all else. He taught me that miracles, and crowds, and salvations, and deliverances were all the fruit and the natural outflow of a genuine life in the Holy Spirit. Pastor Benny taught me that the fruit of walking with the Spirit is to have an addiction for Jesus. He encouraged me to become a Jesus man. While there's no doubt that Benny Hinn knows and loves the Holy Spirit, what most people don't know about him is that he is addicted to Jesus. He is absolutely consumed in prayer with the face of the Lord. This prompted me to seek the depths of the Lord. He taught me that it's never over until God says it's over. He taught me that worshiping the Lord is so much greater than working for the Lord. He let me become close with him, and I am beyond grateful for the privilege. I can honestly tell you that when it comes to discussing the things of God, there's nobody on earth who understands me better—and I would venture to say that the reverse is also true. We see Heaven the same way, and we gaze at the Lord's face the same way.

Benny was used by God to teach me that presence is everything. I will never forget the advice he gave me before I preached my first sermon under his leadership. I was standing behind the curtain, so nervous about what was to come. Before I walked on the platform, he grabbed me and said, "Mikey, just let the people feel the presence of God." He gave me a kiss and pushed me out there. And there I was, in front of a packed building with nothing to do and no plan at all but to let the people feel the presence of God.

Pastor Benny picked me up out of a selfish lifestyle and gave me my start in the ministry. His encouraging words have kept me going when leaders have attacked me and when those I love have distanced themselves from me. He caused me to fight for what I believe in and to never back down off the character of God regardless of the price. Still today I hear him quoting Zechariah to me: "Mikey, 'It's not by might, it's not by power, it's by My Spirit, says the Lord.'" While nobody can teach you how to surrender, he certainly modeled it for me. Today in our meetings around the world all I do is worship the Lord, and listen, and do my best to let Him do whatever the Holy Spirit wants to do. In addition, he let me marry his beautiful daughter! It's hard to top that.

So I want to say, Baba (that's what I call Pastor Benny), thank you for paying a price during that year of glory in 1973. Thank you for spending eight hours a day with the Holy Spirit. Thank you for being infatuated with the One with whom the Holy Spirit is infatuated, Jesus Himself. Thank you for giving your life and your vessel to the Lord. I would not be here without you. I love you so much.

KATHRYN KUHLMAN

As you've undoubtedly discovered by now, my spiritual hero is Kathryn Kuhlman. There's so much I could mention here. What I love about her is that she was more aware of the Holy Spirit than anything or anyone else. While her spiritual work was serious, she found a way to enjoy God while ministering. It was as if Kathryn was caught up into another world. She seemed to minister out of pleasure, delight, and sheer ecstasy. Kathryn was used by God to introduce the Holy Spirit to the world in a beautiful new way. To her, He was not mere fire, force, or power, but He was a real person who could be known and loved.

During a season where men were preaching fire, brimstone, force, and fury, Kathryn came along in elegance and introduced the world to the gentle, holy, reverential, tender Holy Spirit. Many were caught up and distracted by her eclectic, theatrical ways, but there was no denying that when she walked onto the platform, Jesus walked onto that platform with her. This was not a job to Kathryn but a public display of what burned in her heart—oneness with God. She seemed to enjoy the anointing as much as those for whom she was praying.

I own some of Kathryn's ministerial and personal items. They are very precious to me. I met people who worked alongside Kathryn. They all said the same thing: "She was in love with God. She loved His presence more than her calling." I believe that is so vital. That kind of dependence on the Holy Spirit is needed again today. Her respect for His presence is a great model for all of us. She had the ability to let the Holy Spirit have the meeting. While she was not perfect in her day-to-day life, there was no doubt that she loved Him and no doubt that she loved people. I am grateful to Kathryn for teaching us all how to yield to the Holy Spirit and how to enjoy getting to know His beautiful personality.

ORAL ROBERTS

As a young pastor, I lived in Southern California. I was only about fifteen minutes away from Dr. Roberts' house. He was a hero to me because of all the healing breakthrough that he saw. He told the world that God was good and that God still heals today. Oral was used to raise up a generation at Oral Roberts University and to send them to the nations to impact millions for the Kingdom of God. He was a close friend of my father-in-law, and he became a friend of mine. Jessica attended Oral Roberts University, and so did my brother and sister-in-law, Rachel. I was supposed to attend ORU in 1996 on a golf scholarship but decided not to. It was one of the greatest mistakes of my life, and I actually had the chance to tell that to Dr. Roberts.

Early in our ministry, miracles were so rare and scarce. I was praying for people left and right, but nothing was happening. Those were such difficult days. As a pastor, you become one with the pain of your people, and theirs were not minor sicknesses. Some had cancer. Others had kidney disease. A baby was stillborn. I did my best to stand in the gap of these situations. I declared all the Scripture I knew, worshiped, and fasted for these people. Yet none were healed, and I don't know why. I remember being tempted to quit praying for the sick because of all the defeat.

One day, my father-in-law said, "Hey Mikey, come with me to see Oral Roberts." Like a kid in a candy store, I jumped into his car and rode over there with him. I sat there like a little schoolboy, learning from two of faith's greatest heroes. One thing was for sure, though, regardless of who was in the room that day, there was one person in charge—Oral Roberts. He told me and my father-in-law where to sit. He determined what we talked about. He corrected us, rebuked us, loved us, and everything in between. He even challenged us to our faces. I'll never forget the focus and intensity that was on that man. As I sat there, I was amazed by the presence of God that rested on him. Here was the man that God used to bring hope and healing to an entire generation.

After our first meeting, I had the joy of visiting him multiple times. On one occasion, I went over to his church just to check on him. He asked me to move my chair very close to him. We sat face to face, and he poured his heart out to me about the goodness of Jesus. He gave me hope for my future. I'll never forget him telling me, "You can do it. Yes, you can. I am praying for your ministry."

Oral dedicated my firstborn, Theo, to the Lord. He laid hands on me and Jessica and blessed us on more than one occasion. I'm convinced that there was a genuine deposit that took place. He taught me to believe that God is good. He taught me that anything is possible. He instilled in my heart that if you're going to walk with God, you need to make big plans. Faith flowed out of that man. If I have any faith today, he is a part of that inheritance. Thank you, Dr. Roberts, for paying a price and for telling us all who God really is. He is good.

JOY DAWSON

Joy Dawson has been a consistent voice in my life for ten years. As you know from reading this book, Joy and I met at a miracle service in Long Beach, California. That meeting changed my life forever. Since that day, she has stood by my side like a champion, like an immovable rock, challenging me, loving me, and defending me in situations where I could not defend myself. In moments when I did not have the strength or the wisdom to go on, Joy came in and bolstered me, along with her husband, Jim, who's now gone on to be with the Lord. They saw in me what I didn't see in myself. They spoke into being what I only had a hunch to believe in. When I wasn't listening or present, they were telling leaders around the world that God had touched my life and that they should receive me.

Joy has taught me so much—first and foremost, the character of God. The woman is absolutely addicted to the ways and character of God. She loves His wrath as much as His tenderness. She wants Him any way she can have Him, and that's what I love most about her. She has given her life to study and experience who God is. Secondly, she has taught me the fear of the Lord. Nobody I know on planet Earth carries the fear of the Lord like Joy Dawson. The Holy Spirit has used Joy to teach me and show me what it means to fear the Lord. I can feel the increase and wisdom that has come to our family and our movement. And I believe this is because Joy taught us to fear the Lord.

Thirdly, she has modeled how to wait on God. To Joy—and to Jesus, I should say—we do nothing unless we see the Father do it. Joy taught me this very clearly and consistently. Others were running around taking every preaching engagement that came their way, but she would always say to me, "Michael, only go if God tells you to go. Don't make that decision unless God has spoken to you through His Word or through His living voice." What a treasure, what a lifesaver this advice is. Fourthly, she has shown me about revival. Other than Lou Engle, there is nobody I know on earth who is more committed to praying for revival than Joy Dawson. She taught me that there is always more—that regardless of the breakthrough we were seeing, I could believe for more. Joy is believing for the day when the move of the Holy Spirit will sweep every home, nation, church, school, and family. She has been praying for America every Sunday night for one hour for decades. I know God hears her prayers. When America sees the revival that all of us know is coming, let's be sure to thank Joy for standing in the gap all these years.

It is safe to say that there would be no Michael and Jessica or Jesus Image without you, Joy Dawson. Thank you for being an unwavering voice of love and truth in my life. We love you dearly.

BASILEA SCHLINK

Mother Basilea Schlink and her teachings completely turned my world upside down. God used her to rearrange my motives, to turn me into a Mary when I was a Martha. It was her life and the life of the sisters of Mary that illuminated the beautiful truth of the Scripture that "in all we do, do it unto the Lord" (see Col. 3:23). She taught me that first love was the utmost priority. I can still hear her words today: "The only love God receives is first love, and first love is simply returning God's love back to Him."

Mother Basilea branded in my heart that bridal intimacy with Jesus was more important than any other responsibility. She was used by God to show me that Jesus was looking for friends and lovers, that He wants our time, and that our obedience brings Him joy, and our disobedience, pain. She taught me that the sufferings of Jesus could be fellowshipped with. I was shocked to discover that the Lord has pain in His heart when He's rejected and that the Bride could tend to that pain. What a holy calling. No longer would I go into my prayer closet just to pray. I would go in to be with Him, the One who was waiting for me, the One who deeply wanted me.

BILL JOHNSON

From the outside looking in, I can see how many people would think that ministry life is just so easy and fun. While it is fun, it's not always easy. Bill Johnson has been used to convince Jessica and me of the goodness of our Heavenly Father no matter what we're facing. Bill is perhaps the most well-rounded Christian leader I have ever been around. His love for Jesus, revelation of the Scriptures, devotional life, family, marriage, children, church leadership, power and miracles, character, humility, and integrity are as strong as anybody's. Bill has shown us that if we stay humble, we can have as much of God as He has promised.

I love the fact that Bill can walk around his home church as a dad, loving the people. I love watching him as he stays low and humble when there are miracles happening all around him. Bill has been a faithful friend to me and Jessica. Through the many difficult challenges that life has thrown our way, God has used Bill to show us how loving our Father in Heaven is and that the presence of God is still enough. Jesus Image and our family are being transformed by what God has done and is doing in Bill Johnson.

Bill, thank you for loving us, and thank you for telling us that God is still good no matter what we face. Thank you, as well, for encouraging us to say around the world that miracles still happen today. We love you.

REX HUMBARD

In 2003, I met Rex Humbard. What a humble, amazing, meek man. Rex is known as "the father of Christian television." He was also the one who brought Kathryn Kuhlman to Akron, Ohio. He loaned her his tent, and she filled it with thousands. Rex was such a humble, tender man. He had shaken the world in his own right, yet it never seemed to get to his head. The Cathedral of Tomorrow is a mainstay in America. He and his wife, Maude Aimee, were some of our biggest fans. When nobody knew my name, they would tell us that we would change the world for Jesus. He would pray for me and love me and Jessica. Before Jessica and I were ever married, he laid hands on us and said, "Lord, give Michael and Jess what You have given myself and Maude Aimee." We never forgot that prayer and have held on to it for years.

Rex was a holy man and a man full of joy. His son Donny and I became close. Donny would share stories with me when Jessica and I would go down to the assisted living home in South Florida to visit Rex. Did we ever have fun! What a joy and a privilege. Rex loved God, and he loved people. He was a mighty evangelist who could give an altar call like nobody you have ever met. He was very close with Kathryn Kuhlman, and this connection intrigued me greatly.

The day before Rex died, Jesus walked into his room. He saw Him. The Lord said to Rex, "We're ready for you, Rex. It's time to come home." And so, after this experience with the Lord, the doctor came in to give Rex his medication, but Rex clenched his teeth and would not take it. Donny told Rex, "Dad, you have to take your medication." Rex answered, "No, I've seen the Lord. I'm ready to go home." It wasn't very long after that that Rex lay in bed, surrounded by his children, who were singing "Blessed Assurance," when a bolt of lightning hit just outside of Rex's hospital window. The room shook as they continued to sing. Rex sat up in his bed, his face shining like an angel's. Every wrinkle left his face. He looked like he was in his thirties again. He turned to all of his children and smiled, laid back down, and went home to be with the Lord. How can I best sum up Rex Humbard? He was like Jesus.

MADAME GUYON

Our eternal lives should be the most important thing to us on earth. The internal fellowship with the Holy Spirit is our greatest gift. Learning how to commune with the Lord is the greatest lesson we could ever learn. For a time, prayer was a struggle for me. It was full of speaking, requests, trial, and struggle. Then I picked up a book called *Experiencing the Depths of Jesus Christ* by Madame Guyon. She taught me that prayer is simple and easy and that we were created by God to fellowship with the Lord. This fellowship is the most natural thing with which we could ever be involved. She taught me that prayer did not have to begin and end, but it could become a constant experience that is never ending and always increasing. Madame Guyon suffered greatly for her teachings. She died in a prison because she saw that we were all filled with the Spirit and could all commune intimately with God at all times. When somebody changes your prayer life, they change your life. She taught me how to pray, and for that I owe her everything.

REINHARD BONNKE

In 2010, I was going through a very difficult time. My family on Jessica's side had suffered divorce. While I thank God for the restoration that has taken place, the pain of 2010 was very real. I felt like I had been cut off from a life-giving stream that I had had as a boy. It seemed like our world was caving in. Jesus never left, but the challenges increased and increased. I then had the opportunity to get lunch with Reinhard. We sat down at a restaurant in Vero Beach, Florida. He looked across the table and said to me, "You are a man of God in your own right. I feel the power of God when I hear you talking about cities coming to Jesus. You are a man of God." To hear such encouragement from a man that has preached the Gospel face to face to more people than anybody in history was overwhelming. He began to encourage me and lift my faith for nations to come to Jesus. At the same time, I was blown away by the humility in which he walked and by the tenderness in his delivery toward me. It was as if God sent Reinhard as a father in my life when I had felt so rejected by others.

I will never forget the greatest thing he ever told me. In his deep, raspy German voice, he said, "Michael, the crowds in the crusades are not my reward. The presence of Jesus is my reward." I about melted on the table. A man who loved the Holy Spirit more than the work of the ministry—how refreshing. I have never forgotten those words. At the end of the day, His presence is our greatest reward. Reinhard taught me that I did not have to choose between having a character like Jesus and experiencing the power of Jesus. He has declared to the world that coming to Jesus is enough and that He sets the sinner free today.

Reinhard, I want to thank you from the bottom of my heart for embracing me and loving me. Thank you for being like Him.

I hope this chapter stirred you to be grateful for those who have been placed in your life to lead you to the rivers of the Spirit. I hope you'll reach out to them and honor them. I hope you will think about their impact on your life. According to Jesus, when we receive His friends, we receive Him, and when we receive Him, we receive the Father who sent Him (see Matt. 10:40). To receive God's friends is to receive God Himself. Take some time today and honor those whom God has called His friends.

Chapter Twenty-One

IMPARTATION

As I look back on my life with the Holy Spirit, it is absolutely crystal clear to me that I am a recipient of what God gave to others before me. I have been impacted by so many amazing people who knew the Lord deeply. Beyond a shadow of a doubt, my father-in-law, Benny Hinn, has had the greatest spiritual impact on my life. It's safe to say that there would be no Jesus Image and that I would not be in the ministry, born again, or healthy had God not raised up Benny. For that reason, I love him with all my heart. Not to mention he let me marry his daughter thirteen years ago. That's not a bad deal.

So much of what is taking place in Jesus Image and in my life personally is due to an unquestionable impartation that has occurred over the last twenty-seven years. It is amazing to think that God can take what He has given me and what He has given you and share it with others. I've already shared with you how I came to the Lord and was healed in Benny's meetings. As you know, that began years of driving to (and eventually joining) the Orlando Christian Center, his church.

I'd like to take you back to the moment I remember as the first impartation that I received through those meetings and in the life of my father-in-law.

But before we get started, let's talk about impartation and what it is. The Greek word for impartation is *metadidómi*. It means "to give over, to share, to give, to impart." It can also mean "to give a share of." It can mean "to communicate, to relate, to give, or to bestow." It can also mean "to transmit, pass on, or confer, and transfer."

As you read earlier in this book, you'll remember me speaking about that Greek priest, Anthony Morfessis, who walked into the home at the memorial of my uncle and laid hands on my father, healing him instantly. There was such power on that man, and that power was clearly being transmitted to those in the house. As I said, when he walked in, the women began to fall on the floor as he touched them. This was not a church service. This was simply a man visiting a family who was in mourning. You have to understand, we had no background or grid for people falling under the power of God, but I will never forget the sheer power that filled the air. I want to make very clear right now that what I am talking about is the transmission or impartation of the power of the Holy Spirit. I am not focusing on the indwelling of the Holy Spirit. That night with Father Morfessis changed my life. It gave me a taste of what was available in God, and I've never forgotten it.

As the years went on, I came in contact with another cousin of mine named Sam Kalamaras. He was a Greek priest also, and he had received the baptism of the Holy Spirit. I watched him pray for people, and they would be healed. Many of them would fall to the ground, all in the Greek Orthodox Church. Now, for some of you that might sound very common, but for those of you who grew up Catholic or Orthodox, you know what I'm saying is incredibly rare. People typically did not manifest the power of God in those ways in the Orthodox Church. In fact, I had never seen it before. But I would watch my cousin Sam pray for people, and the power of God would flow in an unquestionable way. Of course this amazed me, but I believe God is wanting us to go from amazement to hunger. As these men and women of God show us what's available in God, we have a few options: We can attack what they're doing. We can treat what God is doing through them as being common and average. Or we can realize that God has touched their life in a rare way and be amazed. But I believe that God wants us to take it a step further. Not only does He want us to be amazed and honor what He is doing in them, but He wants it to become an invitation as we discover what's available by looking at these people and what God has given them.

As a young boy, I experienced that with Father Anthony and Father Sam. It caused me to want the power of the Holy Spirit myself. It was Father Sam who took me to my father-in-law's church in 1989, the night I met Jesus, the night I met the Holy Spirit. And as the weeks and months went on, even though I was full of God, enjoying God, and at peace with God, I quickly realized that I needed more. One of the reasons I needed more is because I wanted others to meet the Jesus I had met. I began to learn that I could not force people with my reasoning to give their hearts fully over to Jesus. The Lord was teaching me that I needed the same power that Father Sam had, that Father Anthony had, and that Benny had. I just didn't know how to receive that.

I remember Father Sam's son and the testimony he shared with me when he received the power of the Holy Spirit. The night the power of the Spirit came upon him, he began to speak perfect Hebrew. Father Sam heard a few words while Michael was speaking in tongues, and it sounded like Hebrew to him; so they took him to the rabbi, and the rabbi said that he was quoting a portion of the Book of Isaiah in perfect Hebrew. Our families grew up speaking Greek and English, that's it. Hebrew was not part of our arsenal, that I can promise you. But these stories began to amaze me. These examples began to lure me toward the Lord as I began to discover my own personal need for more of Him.

I began to pray and ask God to touch my life. I was given the book *Good Morning, Holy Spirit*, and the hunger within me multiplied daily as I read the book. Remember, I was only twelve years old, but I would spend hours and hours with God, hours reading the Scriptures, day after day in His presence. *Good Morning, Holy Spirit* introduced me to the person of the Lord in a way that I had never known. I did not know the Holy Spirit could be my friend, and I didn't know that I could speak to Him. This was an amazing time, as hunger began to burn in me. So, as I learned more about the power of the Holy Spirit and God's desire to baptize us in the Holy Spirit, I began to wait on the Lord in my bedroom. Days, weeks, and months went by—still nothing. Being the Greek Orthodox boy that I was, I thought, "Maybe if I put an icon of Jesus in my room, then I'll receive the baptism of the Holy Spirit. After all, John the Baptist said of Jesus, *'He will baptize you with the Holy Spirit and fire'*" (Luke 3:16). Well, at least I knew who the baptizer was. My friend, that's a very important thing to know. Well, the icon didn't do much, for as beautiful as it was, there was still no power. Then I went to the store and bought another icon. This time, it had a candle attached to it. I remember thinking, "Well, if Jesus is the baptizer, and He baptizes us in fire, I've got this thing covered! I've got two in one with this one icon—Jesus, the baptizer, and the fire of the Holy Spirit; the icon and the candle. There's no way I can miss now." I prayed in front of that icon, and nothing happened—not a thing. I'm sure the Lord heard me, but there was no power from on high.

It was during that time that we were driving back and forth between Tarpon Springs and Orlando to attend Benny's meetings. We attended a Sunday night meeting, and following the meeting, he announced, "This coming Wednesday night I will be teaching on the baptism of the Holy Spirit." I looked at my mom and said, "We're coming," and so we did. He began to talk about much of what I've been talking to you about in this book, but it was specifically about receiving the power of the Holy Spirit. As he began to teach the Scriptures that Wednesday night, I could feel something happening inside of me. I could feel faith like I had never felt before, and I knew that this Wednesday night was my night.

Following the teaching, he looked at the crowd and said, "If you want to receive the baptism of the Holy Spirit, run up here right now," and so I did. I was in maybe the third row and ran straight to that altar. It was complete chaos and pandemonium. Hundreds of people came forward. I'm sure many of them had already received the baptism of the Holy Spirit, but they were just hungry for more. Maybe some of them were even lying, who knows; I couldn't care less. All I knew is that this was my night, the night I had been waiting for, for about a year. Before I knew it, I heard a voice say, "Hey, bring that young boy up here." By this time, my father-in-law and I had connected, spoken, and spent time together at the church. He knew who I was, and so he said, "Get that boy up here. I want to pray for him." All I can remember is him moving toward me. The next thing I knew, I was on the floor. A power began to flow through my body, at which point I felt the most beautiful touch on my tongue, and from my mouth—without trying at all and without anybody coaching me—the most beautiful sounds began to flow.

I was still conscious, and I remember thinking, "How can this be happening to me? This is incredible. This is what I've been waiting for." The sounds began to flow and flow, and they would turn into songs. The most beautiful notes and spiritual beauty began to flow out of my mouth and through my body. I shook and shook under the power of the Holy Spirit. Yes, I had received Jesus already. Yes, I had felt His healing touch, but this was different. This felt like ecstatic power. The ability to worship the Lord became completely natural. I felt absolute joy. It was as though I had been lifted to another place, another world. It literally felt like I was swimming in a river of absolute delight, like I had been thrown into the person of the Holy Spirit. My friend, I had. The word *baptism* means "to be thrust into," and that's exactly what had happened. Jesus had grabbed me and plunged me into the invisible river of the Spirit of God. That glorious power took over my body and began to use my mouth as an instrument of praise and declaration of who God is and how wonderful He will forever be. I will never forget this moment as long as I live. I probably spent about two hours on the ground that night shaking.

You might enjoy knowing this: Twenty years later, Jessica asked me, "When were you baptized in the Holy Spirit?" And I told her. I described the service to her. I told her who was on the platform next to me, also being filled with the Holy Spirit. She said, "That's the night I was filled with the Holy Spirit and began to speak in tongues." After our discussion, it was clear that when I was twelve years old and she was eight, God had made sure that we would be both filled with the Holy Spirit on the same night. How amazing is the Lord?

You say, "Well, what happened that night? Why did God wait for that service to fill you with the Spirit after you had spent weeks and months in your room alone with Him?" Well, first of all, time alone with Jesus is never wasted. I believe God began to prepare my heart, teach me to pray, and also reveal my need for Him. You know, prayer without the power of the Spirit will wear you down. Those weeks and months in prayer revealed to me that I needed God for everything. I believe that the power of the Spirit is transferrable. It can be imparted. For some reason, what God had given to Benny to carry, the Lord decided to release on me that night as a young boy.

It's important we understand that while God will use men and women as instruments of impartation, all that we receive comes from the Lord. In John 1:16, the Bible says it is *"of His fullness we have all received...."* Again, Jesus told the disciples, *"...[Wait] in the city of Jerusalem until you are endued with power from on high"* (Luke 24:49). That

Scripture highlights so much, but the portion that I believe we often miss is this: The power must come from on high. Michael's power will do nothing for you. Benny's power will do nothing for you. Father Sam's and Anthony's power will do nothing for you. But Jesus' power will. So, the power must come from on high because that's where Jesus is. He is the baptizer of the Holy Spirit. Never forget that every good gift comes down from above (see James 1:17). We can never take credit or give man the credit for what flows from God alone. While we should honor, we must forever remember the source: Jesus Himself.

That night, Benny laid hands on me. God had decided that I would be filled with the Spirit in this way. This is in the Scriptures. Romans 1:11-12 says, *"For I long to see you, that I may impart to you some spiritual gift to make you strong—that is, that you and I may be mutually encouraged by each other's faith"* (NIV).

The Samaritan believers received the Holy Spirit as a result of Peter and John laying hands on them. Acts 8:14-17 says,

> *When the apostles back in Jerusalem heard that the people of Samaria had accepted God's message, they sent Peter and John there. As soon as they arrived, they prayed for these new believers to receive the Holy Spirit. The Holy Spirit had not yet come upon any of them, for they had only been baptized in the name of the Lord Jesus. Then Peter and John laid their hands upon these believers, and they received the Holy Spirit"*(NLT).

What a beautiful picture of the Holy Spirit's work in us!

Remember when Jesus breathed on the disciples in John 20:22 and said, *"Receive the Holy Spirit"*—it was at that moment that they were born again and saved. It was also the moment that the Holy Spirit began to live on the inside of them and filled their spirits. They became the temple of the Holy Spirit. This is called the indwelling of the Holy Spirit, the presence of God within us. Every born-again Christian is filled with the Holy Spirit. I am talking about something entirely different. I am referring to what Jesus was talking about in Acts 1:8 when He said, *"Ye shall receive power, after that the Holy Spirit is come upon you"* (KJV). The moment He comes upon us, power is ours, and that is what I am talking about right now.

These Samaritan believers had already received Jesus as the indwelling Lord, by the Holy Spirit, but they had yet to be empowered to live the Christian life. I love the way Bill Johnson says it: "He is in me for me and on me for you." This is very true. The Holy Spirit within us connects us with the Lord, gives us the opportunity to fellowship with Jesus at any time and any place. He is a fountain of living water on the inside, no matter where we go. But the Holy Spirit on us empowers us to break the power of the devil off of those who desperately need Jesus. The Bible says, "It is the anointing (or the smearing of power) that breaks the yoke" (see Isa. 10:27). This is exactly what happened to me on that rainy night in 1989. I had already been saved, but now God would give me the power to bring that saving touch to those I loved and desperately wanted to know Jesus.

Acts 9:17-20 beautifully describes the apostle Paul's experience. It says,

Ananias went his way, and entered into the house; and putting his hands on him said, Brother Saul, the Lord, even Jesus, that appeared unto thee in the way as thou camest, hath sent me, that thou mightest receive thy sight, and be filled with the Holy Ghost. And immediately there fell from his eyes as it had been scales: and he received sight forthwith, and arose, and was baptized.... And straightway he preached Christ in the synagogues, that He is the Son of God (Acts 9:17-18,20 KJV).

As a result of Ananias laying hands on Saul, there was absolutely a transfer of the power of the Holy Spirit in Saul's life. We would call this the baptism of the Holy Spirit. Remember, Saul came to the

Lord on the road to Damascus, but he was not ready to share Jesus and preach the Gospel in the way that Jesus did without having the same power that Jesus had. Notice it was after Ananias laid hands on Paul and he received the power of the Holy Spirit that *"he preached Christ in the synagogues, that He is the Son of God"* (Acts 9:20). Was Ananias the source? No, he was the channel of Jesus the baptizer.

In Ephesus, the apostle Paul did exactly what Ananias did to him. Acts 19:6 says, *"And when Paul laid his hands upon them, the Holy Ghost came on them; and they spake with tongues, and prophesied"* (KJV). These believers were released in a completely new world in the Holy Spirit, receiving the gift of prophecy and the ability to speak with new tongues. The gifts of the Holy Spirit can also be transferred through impartation and the laying on of hands. The apostle Paul said to his son in the faith, Timothy, *"Neglect not the gift that is in thee, which was given thee by prophecy, with the laying on of hands of the* [elders]. *Meditate upon these things; give thyself wholly to them; that thy profiting may appear to all"* (1 Tim. 4:14-15 KJV). This is impartation. The gifts that Paul and the elders carried were imparted to Timothy. In Second Timothy 1:6, Paul reminds Timothy again, *"Wherefore I put thee in remembrance that thou stir up the gift of God, which is in thee by the putting on of my hands"* (KJV).

In Acts 6, the Bible says, *"...and when they prayed, they laid their hands on them. And the Word of God increased..."* (Acts 6:6-7 KJV). This laying on of hands produced great power in the life of Stephen. The Bible says, *"Stephen, full of faith and power, did great wonders and miracles among the people"* (Acts 6:8 KJV). The Greek word for power is *dunamis*. It means "natural capability, power, capability to do anything, ability to perform anything, absolutely nothing is impossible, complete power and action." Something happened in the life of Stephen when the apostles laid hands on him.

The Spirit of wisdom and revelation and a new calling can be transferred by the laying on of hands and impartation. The Bible says:

Then Moses spoke to the Lord, saying: "Let the Lord, the God of the spirits of all flesh, set a man over the congregation, who may go out before them and go in before them, who may lead them out and bring them in, that the congregation of the Lord may not be like sheep which have no shepherd." And the Lord said to Moses: "Take Joshua the son of Nun with you, a man in whom is the Spirit, and lay your hand on him; set him before Eleazar the priest and before all the congregation, and inaugurate him in their sight. And you shall give some of your authority to him, that all the congregation of the children of Israel may be obedient. He shall stand before Eleazar the priest, who shall inquire before the Lord for him by the judgment of the Urim. At his word they shall go out, and at his word they shall come in, he and all the children of Israel with him—all the congregation." So Moses did as the Lord commanded him. He took Joshua and set him before Eleazar the priest and before all the congregation. And he laid his hands on him and inaugurated him, just as the Lord commanded by the hand of Moses. (Numbers 27:15-23).

Notice Moses imparted honor and authority. Those Hebrew words mean "beauty, brilliance, grandeur, excellence, glory, honor." This impartation gave Joshua a spiritual credibility to which the people responded. In Deuteronomy 34, we see that Joshua received an impartation of wisdom from the hands of Moses. It says in verse 9: *"Joshua the son of Nun was full of the spirit of wisdom; for Moses had laid his hands upon him: and the children of Israel hearkened unto him, and did as the Lord commanded Moses"* (Deut. 34:9 KJV). Just think, Joshua left with heavenly wisdom after God's servant prayed for him.

If you trace revival history and study the lives of those who have shaken the world, all of them had been impacted by those who went before them and by those who lived among them. Reinhard Bonnke is a dear friend of mine and somebody whom I look up to so much. You'd have to search the world through to find a man like Reinhard. Many times, over a meal, or over a private time of fellowship, Reinhard shares the stories of when George Jeffreys, the great English revivalist, laid hands on him. Reinhard left that place completely changed—"full of the glory of God," Reinhard said.

I have spoken to those who have told me that Aimee Semple McPherson was used in the life of Kathryn Kuhlman. F. F. Bosworth helped Maria Woodworth-Etter in her meetings. Lester Sumrall was deeply impacted by the life of Smith Wigglesworth. Benny Hinn was touched by the life of Kathryn Kuhlman. Bill Johnson was deeply impacted by John Wimber and the Toronto Blessing. Steve Hill was touched by the Argentine Revival and the ministry of Pastor Benny. Heidi Baker was changed in the revival meeting in Toronto. The point is this: While everything comes from the Lord, the Lord has decided to use His friends to give away what God has given them.

While I cannot give you everything I have, I can pray and ask that an impartation live in this book and that impartation of the power of the Holy Spirit will come on you now and change your life. This is what I am believing for you: Number one, that through this impartation, the presence of God would be more real to you than ever; number two, that an anointing to pray and spend time with Jesus would be yours; number three, that the love of God would flow in you and through you; number four, that you would break the power of the devil off of people's lives, and that mighty miracles, signs, and wonders would flow through you; number five, that the declaration of the Gospel would come out of your mouth like fire; and number six, that all of your family and friends would receive what you're about to receive right now.

Let's pray.

Heavenly Father, I come to You needy; I need You, Lord. You said that I could ask You for anything in the name of Jesus, and so I come, asking for an impartation of what rests in this book and on this ministry. Holy Spirit, I need You. Jesus, I receive the power, the favor, the wisdom, and every gift of the Holy Spirit that You have for me now, in Jesus' name, amen.

Chapter Twenty-Two

WORD AND SPIRIT

HIS WORD, HIS SPIRIT, AND YOU

The Word of God reveals the person and work of the Holy Spirit a billion times better than I ever could. Remember, His voice flows from His presence. It is also wrapped in His presence. It is impossible to separate God's Word, voice, and person. Let's have a look at what the Scriptures have to say about this. In Exodus 3, the Bible provides a life-changing truth:

> *The angel of the Lord appeared to him in a blazing fire from the midst of a bush; and he looked, and behold, the bush was burning with fire, yet the bush was not consumed. So Moses said, "I must turn aside now and see this marvelous sight, why the bush is not burned up." When the Lord saw that he turned aside to look, God called to him from the midst of the bush and said, "Moses, Moses!" And he said, "Here I am." Then He said, "Do not come near here; remove your sandals from your feet, for the place on which you*

are standing is holy ground." He said also, "I am the God of your father, the God of Abraham, the God of Isaac, and the God of Jacob." Then Moses hid his face, for he was afraid to look at God (Exodus 3:2-6 NASB).

Notice in verse 4 that the voice of the Lord came from the midst of the bush (see Exod. 3:4). When you combine that truth with the words of Jesus in John 6, "My words are spirit...," we experience a beautiful revelation (see John 6:63). His voice flows from Him and is full of Him. Think of it this way: To hear God, I must come to God, and His voice is wrapped in His Spirit. Once you discover this, you'll never read the Scriptures the same way again! You won't come to your Bible anymore. You will come to Jesus through your Bible. You'll begin to look at every verse as a living moment in the Holy Spirit. The Bible was never meant to be merely read. Rather, it was intended to be seen, heard, felt, meditated on, and consumed. When you sit down and invite the Holy Spirit to teach you and lead you as you read the Scriptures, you will begin to experience His breath, which is His voice.

As my friend Eric Gilmour says, "His voice comes from His mouth, and His mouth is in His face." Wow! To experience the Word of God is to sit before the face of Jesus.

Have you ever tried to speak without breathing? Unless there is the release of breath, we cannot make a sound. When God speaks in His Word, He releases His breath, the Holy Spirit!

The Bible says it is *"out of the abundance of the heart* [that] *the mouth speaks"* (Matt. 12:34). This is amazing. Remember, even though Jesus said this to others, it also reveals to us how He works. More specifically, it gives us a beautiful picture of His internal workings. So, think of this for a moment: Whatever Jesus says is a revelation of His heart. I like to say it this way: "The Bible is God's heart on paper." Unlike us at times, Jesus doesn't "just say things" and not mean what He says. He is pure truth. That means that His heart is on full display in the Word. What a privilege to see Him this way!

- To love the Word of God is to love God's voice, which is Spirit.
- To love the Word of God is to love His face, from which the voice flows.
- To love the Word of God is to love God's breath, which is the Holy Spirit Himself.
- To love the Word of God is to love His heart.

The other side of the coin is:

- To not love the Word is to not love the voice of God, which is Spirit.
- To not love the Spirit is to not love His face, from which the voice flows.
- To not love the Word is to not love the breath of God, which is the Holy Spirit.
- To not love the Word is to not love His heart.

THE HOLY SPIRIT IN SCRIPTURE

As you read the pure truth of the Scriptures, I believe your heart and mind will open into a fresh revelation of the beauty and power of the Spirit. Encounter belongs to you, as you read these amazing verses from God's Word.[1] Let's have a look at what the Bible has to say about the Holy Spirit. My prayer is that this chapter will be a resource for you and your family as you walk in deep friendship with the Holy Spirit.

Spirit of the Father

For it is not you who speak, but it is the Spirit of your Father who speaks in you (Matthew 10:20).

For He whom God has sent speaks the words of God; for He gives the Spirit without measure (John 3:34).

When the Helper comes, whom I will send to you from the Father, that is the Spirit of truth who proceeds from the Father, He will testify about Me (John 15:26).

Therefore having been exalted to the right hand of God, and having received from the Father the promise of the Holy Spirit, He has poured forth this which you both see and hear (Acts 2:33).

For all who are being led by the Spirit of God, these are sons of God (Romans 8:14).

For you have not received a spirit of slavery leading to fear again, but you have received a spirit of adoption as sons by which we cry out, "Abba! Father!" (Romans 8:15).

The Spirit Himself testifies with our spirit that we are children of God (Romans 8:16).

And not only this, but also we ourselves, having the first fruits of the Spirit, even we ourselves groan within ourselves, waiting eagerly for our adoption as sons, the redemption of our body (Romans 8:23).

Who also sealed us and gave us the Spirit in our hearts as a pledge (2 Corinthians 1:22).

Now He who prepared us for this very purpose is God, who gave to us the Spirit as a pledge (2 Corinthians 5:5).

For through Him we both have our access in one Spirit to the Father (Ephesians 2:18).

Spirit of Jesus

And Jesus, crying out with a loud voice, said, "Father, into Your hands I commit My spirit." Having said this, He breathed His last (Luke 23:46).

When the Helper comes, whom I will send to you from the Father, that is the Spirit of truth who proceeds from the Father, He will testify about Me (John 15:26).

And after they came to Mysia, they were trying to go into Bithynia, and the Spirit of Jesus did not permit them (Acts 16:7).

Therefore I make known to you that no one speaking by the Spirit of God says, "Jesus is accursed"; and no one can say, "Jesus is Lord," except by the Holy Spirit (1 Corinthians 12:3).

For I know that this will turn out for my deliverance through your prayers and the provision of the Spirit of Jesus Christ (Philippians 1:19).

By this you know the Spirit of God: every spirit that confesses that Jesus Christ has come in the flesh is from God (1 John 4:2).

Then I fell at his feet to worship him. But he said to me, "Do not do that; I am a fellow servant of yours and your brethren who hold the testimony of Jesus; worship God. For the testimony of Jesus is the spirit of prophecy" (Revelation 19:10).

God

The earth was formless and void, and darkness was over the surface of the deep, and the Spirit of God was moving over the surface of the waters (Genesis 1:2).

Then Pharaoh said to his servants, "Can we find a man like this, in whom is a divine spirit? (Genesis 41:38).

Then the Lord said, "My Spirit shall not strive with man forever, because he also is flesh; nevertheless his days shall be one hundred and twenty years" (Genesis 6:3).

If He should determine to do so, if He should gather to Himself His spirit and His breath (Job 34:14).

The Spirit of God has made me, and the breath of the Almighty gives me life (Job 33:4).

The Spirit of the Lord will rest on Him… (Isaiah 11:2).

Who has directed the Spirit of the Lord, or as His counselor has informed Him? (Isaiah 40:13).

And now the Lord God has sent Me, and His Spirit (Isaiah 48:16).

O Belteshazzar, chief of the magicians, since I know that a spirit of the holy gods is in you and no mystery baffles you, tell me the visions of my dream which I have seen, along with its interpretation (Daniel 4:9).

This is the dream which I, King Nebuchadnezzar, have seen. Now you, Belteshazzar, tell me its interpretation, inasmuch as none of the wise men of my kingdom is able to make known to me the interpretation; but you are able, for a spirit of the holy gods is in you (Daniel 4:18).

There is a man in your kingdom in whom is a spirit of the holy gods; and in the days of your father, illumination, insight and wisdom like the wisdom of the gods were found in him. And King Nebuchadnezzar, your father, your father the king, appointed him chief of the magicians, conjurers, Chaldeans and diviners (Daniel 5:11).

Then he said to me, "This is the word of the Lord to Zerubbabel saying, 'Not by might nor by power, but by My Spirit,' says the Lord of hosts" (Zechariah 4:6).

Then Jesus was led up by the Spirit into the wilderness to be tempted by the devil (Matthew 4:1).

Therefore I say to you, any sin and blasphemy shall be forgiven people, but blasphemy against the Spirit shall not be forgiven (Matthew 12:31).

Whoever speaks a word against the Son of Man, it shall be forgiven him; but whoever speaks against the Holy Spirit, it shall not be forgiven him, either in this age or in the age to come (Matthew 12:32).

Go therefore and make disciples of all the nations, baptizing them in the name of the Father and the Son and the Holy Spirit (Matthew 28:19).

The angel answered and said to her, "The Holy Spirit will come upon you, and the power of the Most High will overshadow you; and for that reason the holy Child shall be called the Son of God (Luke 1:35).

God is spirit, and those who worship Him must worship in spirit and truth (John 4:24).

But Peter said, "Ananias, why has satan filled your heart to lie to the Holy Spirit and to keep back some of the price of the land?" (Acts 5:3).

Then Peter said to her, "Why is it that you have agreed together to put the Spirit of the Lord to the test? Behold, the feet of those who have buried your husband are at the door, and they will carry you out as well" (Acts 5:9).

And after they came to Mysia, they were trying to go into Bithynia, and the Spirit of Jesus did not permit them (Acts 16:7).

For the law of the Spirit of life in Christ Jesus has set you free from the law of sin and of death (Romans 8:2).

For to us God revealed them through the Spirit; for the Spirit searches all things, even the depths of God (1 Corinthians 2:10).

For who among men knows the thoughts of a man except the spirit of the man which is in him? Even so the thoughts of God no one knows except the Spirit of God (1 Corinthians 2:11).

Now we have received, not the spirit of the world, but the Spirit who is from God, so that we may know the things freely given to us by God (1 Corinthians 2:12).

Such were some of you; but you were washed, but you were sanctified, but you were justified in the name of the Lord Jesus Christ and in the Spirit of our God (1 Corinthians 6:11).

But in my opinion she is happier if she remains as she is; and I think that I also have the Spirit of God (1 Corinthians 7:40).

So also it is written, "The first man, Adam, became a living soul." The last Adam became a life-giving spirit (1 Corinthians 15:45).

Now the Lord is the Spirit, and where the Spirit of the Lord is, there is liberty (2 Corinthians 3:17).

But we all, with unveiled face, beholding as in a mirror the glory of the Lord, are being transformed into the same image from glory to glory, just as from the Lord, the Spirit (2 Corinthians 3:18).

If we live by the Spirit, let us also walk by the Spirit (Galatians 5:25).

So, he who rejects this is not rejecting man but the God who gives His Holy Spirit to you (1 Thessalonians 4:8).

There is one body and one Spirit, just as also you were called in one hope of your calling (Ephesians 4:4).

For we are the true circumcision, who worship in the Spirit of God and glory in Christ Jesus and put no confidence in the flesh (Philippians 3:3).

By common confession, great is the mystery of godliness: He who was revealed in the flesh, was vindicated in the Spirit, seen by angels, proclaimed among the nations, believed on in the world, taken up in glory (1 Timothy 3:16).

By this you know the Spirit of God: every spirit that confesses that Jesus Christ has come in the flesh is from God (1 John 4:2).

Your Teacher

The Spirit of the Lord will rest on Him...the spirit of counsel and strength, the spirit of knowledge and the fear of the Lord (Isaiah 11:2).

And it had been revealed to him by the Holy Spirit that he would not see death before he had seen the Lord's Christ (Luke 2:26).

For the Holy Spirit will teach you in that very hour what you ought to say (Luke 12:12).

But the Spirit explicitly says that in later times some will fall away from the faith, paying attention to deceitful spirits and doctrines of demons (1 Timothy 4:1).

Guide

And he came in the Spirit into the temple; and when the parents brought in the child Jesus, to carry out for Him the custom of the Law (Luke 2:27).

Jesus, full of the Holy Spirit, returned from the Jordan and was led around by the Spirit in the wilderness (Luke 4:1).

Then the Spirit said to Philip, "Go up and join this chariot" (Acts 8:29).

The Spirit told me to go with them without misgivings. These six brethren also went with me and we entered the man's house (Acts 11:12).

For it seemed good to the Holy Spirit and to us to lay upon you no greater burden than these essentials (Acts 15:28).

They passed through the Phrygian and Galatian region, having been forbidden by the Holy Spirit to speak the word in Asia (Acts 16:6).

Except that the Holy Spirit solemnly testifies to me in every city, saying that bonds and afflictions await me (Acts 20:23).

After looking up the disciples, we stayed there seven days; and they kept telling Paul through the Spirit not to set foot in Jerusalem (Acts 21:4).

And coming to us, he took Paul's belt and bound his own feet and hands, and said, "This is what the Holy Spirit says: 'In this way the Jews at Jerusalem will bind the man who owns this belt and deliver him into the hands of the Gentiles'" (Acts 21:11).

For all who are being led by the Spirit of God, these are sons of God (Romans 8:14).

Therefore, just as the Holy Spirit says, "Today if you hear His voice" (Hebrews 3:7).

Spirit of Wisdom and Revelation

I have filled him with the Spirit of God in wisdom, in understanding, in knowledge, and in all kinds of craftsmanship (Exodus 31:3).

You shall speak to all the skillful persons whom I have endowed with the spirit of wisdom, that they make Aaron's garments to consecrate him, that he may minister as priest to Me (Exodus 28:3).

And He has filled him with the Spirit of God, in wisdom, in understanding and in knowledge and in all craftsmanship (Exodus 35:31).

Now Joshua the son of Nun was filled with the spirit of wisdom, for Moses had laid his hands on him; and the sons of Israel listened to him and did as the Lord had commanded Moses (Deuteronomy 34:9).

You gave Your good Spirit to instruct them, Your manna You did not withhold from their mouth, and You gave them water for their thirst (Nehemiah 9:20).

The Spirit of the Lord will rest on Him, the spirit of wisdom and understanding, the spirit of counsel and strength, the spirit of knowledge and the fear of the Lord (Isaiah 11:2).

This was because an extraordinary spirit, knowledge and insight, interpretation of dreams, explanation of enigmas and solving of difficult problems were found in this Daniel, whom the king named Belteshazzar. Let Daniel now be summoned and he will declare the interpretation (Daniel 5:12).

Now I have heard about you that a spirit of the gods is in you, and that illumination, insight and extraordinary wisdom have been found in you (Daniel 5:14).

Then this Daniel began distinguishing himself among the commissioners and satraps because he possessed an extraordinary spirit, and the king planned to appoint him over the entire kingdom (Daniel 6:3).

Therefore, brethren, select from among you seven men of good reputation, full of the Spirit and of wisdom, whom we may put in charge of this task (Acts 6:3).

Which things we also speak, not in words taught by human wisdom, but in those taught by the Spirit, combining spiritual thoughts with spiritual words (1 Corinthians 2:13).

But a natural man does not accept the things of the Spirit of God, for they are foolishness to him; and he cannot understand them, because they are spiritually appraised (1 Corinthians 2:14).

That the God of our Lord Jesus Christ, the Father of glory, may give to you a spirit of wisdom and of revelation in the knowledge of Him (Ephesians 1:17).

But they were unable to cope with the wisdom and the Spirit with which he was speaking (Acts 6:10).

For to one is given the word of wisdom through the Spirit, and to another the word of knowledge according to the same Spirit (1 Corinthians 12:8).

For one who speaks in a tongue does not speak to men but to God; for no one understands, but in his spirit he speaks mysteries (1 Corinthians 14:2).

Spirit of Life

Of all that was on the dry land, all in whose nostrils was the breath of the spirit of life, died (Genesis 7:22).

The Spirit of God has made me, and the breath of the Almighty gives me life (Job 33:4).

Do not cast me away from Your presence and do not take Your Holy Spirit from me (Psalm 51:11).

You send forth Your Spirit, they are created; and You renew the face of the ground (Psalm 104:30).

Thus says God the Lord, who created the heavens and stretched them out, who spread out the earth and its offspring, who gives breath to the people on it and spirit to those who walk in it (Isaiah 42:5).

Wherever the spirit was about to go, they would go in that direction. And the wheels rose close beside them; for the spirit of the living beings was in the wheels (Ezekiel 1:20).

Whenever those went, these went; and whenever those stood still, these stood still. And whenever those rose from the earth, the wheels rose close beside them; for the spirit of the living beings was in the wheels (Ezekiel 1:21).

When the cherubim stood still, the wheels would stand still; and when they rose up, the wheels would rise with them, for the spirit of the living beings was in them (Ezekiel 10:17).

And I will give them one heart, and put a new spirit within them. And I will take the heart of stone out of their flesh and give them a heart of flesh (Ezekiel 11:19).

Cast away from you all your transgressions which you have committed and make yourselves a new heart and a new spirit! For why will you die, O house of Israel? (Ezekiel 18:31).

I will put My Spirit within you and cause you to walk in My statutes, and you will be careful to observe My ordinances (Ezekiel 36:27).

"I will put My Spirit within you and you will come to life, and I will place you on your own land. Then you will know that I, the Lord, have spoken and done it," declares the Lord (Ezekiel 37:14).

Now the birth of Jesus Christ was as follows: when His mother Mary had been betrothed to Joseph, before they came together she was found to be with child by the Holy Spirit (Matthew 1:18).

But when he had considered this, behold, an angel of the Lord appeared to him in a dream, saying, "Joseph, son of David, do not be afraid to take Mary as your wife; for the Child who has been conceived in her is of the Holy Spirit" (Matthew 1:20).

Jesus answered, "Truly, truly, I say to you, unless one is born of water and the Spirit he cannot enter into the kingdom of God" (John 3:5).

That which is born of the flesh is flesh, and that which is born of the Spirit is spirit (John 3:6).

The wind blows where it wishes and you hear the sound of it, but do not know where it comes from and where it is going; so is everyone who is born of the Spirit (John 3:8).

But an hour is coming, and now is, when the true worshipers will worship the Father in spirit and truth; for such people the Father seeks to be His worshipers (John 4:23).

It is the Spirit who gives life; the flesh profits nothing; the words that I have spoken to you are spirit and are life (John 6:63).

And when He had said this, He breathed on them and said to them, "Receive the Holy Spirit" (John 20:22).

Who was declared the Son of God with power by the resurrection from the dead, according to the Spirit of holiness, Jesus Christ our Lord (Romans 1:4).

But he is a Jew who is one inwardly; and circumcision is that which is of the heart, by the Spirit, not by the letter; and his praise is not from men, but from God (Romans 2:29).

But now we have been released from the Law, having died to that by which we were bound, so that we serve in newness of the Spirit and not in oldness of the letter (Romans 7:6).

So that the requirement of the Law might be fulfilled in us, who do not walk according to the flesh but according to the Spirit (Romans 8:4).

For those who are according to the flesh set their minds on the things of the flesh, but those who are according to the Spirit, the things of the Spirit (Romans 8:5).

For the mind set on the flesh is death, but the mind set on the Spirit is life and peace (Romans 8:6).

However, you are not in the flesh but in the Spirit, if indeed the Spirit of God dwells in you. But if anyone does not have the Spirit of Christ, he does not belong to Him (Romans 8:9).

But if the Spirit of Him who raised Jesus from the dead dwells in you, He who raised Christ Jesus from the dead will also give life to your mortal bodies through His Spirit who dwells in you (Romans 8:11).

For if you are living according to the flesh, you must die; but if by the Spirit you are putting to death the deeds of the body, you will live (Romans 8:13).

Being manifested that you are a letter of Christ, cared for by us, written not with ink but with the Spirit of the living God, not on tablets of stone but on tablets of human hearts (2 Corinthians 3:3).

Who also made us adequate as servants of a new covenant, not of the letter but of the Spirit; for the letter kills, but the Spirit gives life (2 Corinthians 3:6).

Are you so foolish? Having begun by the Spirit, are you now being perfected by the flesh? (Galatians 3:3).

Because you are sons, God has sent forth the Spirit of His Son into our hearts, crying, "Abba! Father!" (Galatians 4:6).

But as at that time he who was born according to the flesh persecuted him who was born according to the Spirit, so it is now also (Galatians 4:29).

But I say, walk by the Spirit, and you will not carry out the desire of the flesh (Galatians 5:16).

For the flesh sets its desire against the Spirit, and the Spirit against the flesh; for these are in opposition to one another, so that you may not do the things that you please (Galatians 5:17).

But if you are led by the Spirit, you are not under the Law (Galatians 5:18).

For the one who sows to his own flesh will from the flesh reap corruption, but the one who sows to the Spirit will from the Spirit reap eternal life (Galatians 6:8).

In whom you also are being built together into a dwelling of God in the Spirit (Ephesians 2:22).

Guard, through the Holy Spirit who dwells in us, the treasure which has been entrusted to you (2 Timothy 1:14).

He saved us, not on the basis of deeds which we have done in righteousness, but according to His mercy, by the washing of regeneration and renewing by the Holy Spirit (Titus 3:5).

Seeking to know what person or time the Spirit of Christ within them was indicating as He predicted the sufferings of Christ and the glories to follow (1 Peter 1:11).

For Christ also died for sins once for all, the just for the unjust, so that He might bring us to God, having been put to death in the flesh, but made alive in the spirit (1 Peter 3:18).

By this we know that we abide in Him and He in us, because He has given us of His Spirit (1 John 4:13).

The one who keeps His commandments abides in Him, and He in him. We know by this that He abides in us, by the Spirit whom He has given us (1 John 3:24).

For the gospel has for this purpose been preached even to those who are dead, that though they are judged in the flesh as men, they may live in the spirit according to the will of God (1 Peter 4:6).

Spirit upon You and Filling You

Then I will come down and speak with you there, and I will take of the Spirit who is upon you, and will put Him upon them; and they shall bear the burden of the people with you, so that you will not bear it all alone (Numbers 11:17).

Then the Lord came down in the cloud and spoke to him; and He took of the Spirit who was upon him and placed Him upon the seventy elders. And when the Spirit rested upon them, they prophesied. But they did not do it again (Numbers 11:25).

But two men had remained in the camp; the name of one was Eldad and the name of the other Medad. And the Spirit rested upon them (now they were among those who had been registered, but had not gone out to the tent), and they prophesied in the camp (Numbers 11:26).

But Moses said to him, "Are you jealous for my sake? Would that all the Lord's people were prophets, that the Lord would put His Spirit upon them!" (Numbers 11:29).

And Balaam lifted up his eyes and saw Israel camping tribe by tribe; and the Spirit of God came upon him (Numbers 24:2).

So the Lord said to Moses, "Take Joshua the son of Nun, a man in whom is the Spirit, and lay your hand on him" (Numbers 27:18).

Then the Spirit of the Lord will come upon you mightily, and you shall prophesy with them and be changed into another man (1 Samuel 10:6).

And the Spirit of the Lord began to stir him in Mahaneh-dan, between Zorah and Eshtaol (Judges 13:25).

Then Samuel took the horn of oil and anointed him in the midst of his brothers; and the Spirit of the Lord came mightily upon David from that day forward. And Samuel arose and went to Ramah (1 Samuel 16:13).

When they had crossed over, Elijah said to Elisha, "Ask what I shall do for you before I am taken from you." And Elisha said, "Please, let a double portion of your spirit be upon me" (2 Kings 2:9).

Now when the sons of the prophets who were at Jericho opposite him saw him, they said, "The spirit of Elijah rests on Elisha." And they came to meet him and bowed themselves to the ground before him (2 Kings 2:15).

Then the Spirit came upon Amasai, who was the chief of the thirty, and he said... (1 Chronicles 12:18).

Now the Spirit of God came on Azariah the son of Oded (2 Chronicles 15:1).

Then in the midst of the assembly the Spirit of the Lord came upon Jahaziel the son of Zechariah, the son of Benaiah, the son of Jeiel, the son of Mattaniah, the Levite of the sons of Asaph (2 Chronicles 20:14).

Then the Spirit of God came on Zechariah the son of Jehoiada the priest; and he stood above the people and said to them, "Thus God has said, 'Why do you transgress the commandments of the Lord and do not prosper? Because you have forsaken the Lord, He has also forsaken you'" (2 Chronicles 24:20).

Turn to my reproof, behold, I will pour out my spirit on you; I will make my words known to you (Proverbs 1:23).

So the Spirit of the Lord came upon Gideon; and he blew a trumpet, and the Abiezrites were called together to follow him (Judges 6:34).

Until the Spirit is poured out upon us from on high, and the wilderness becomes a fertile field, and the fertile field is considered as a forest (Isaiah 32:15).

"As for Me, this is My covenant with them," says the Lord: "My Spirit which is upon you, and My words which I have put in your mouth shall not depart from your mouth, nor from the mouth of your offspring, nor from the mouth of your offspring's offspring," says the Lord, "from now and forever" (Isaiah 59:21).

As for me, I baptize you with water for repentance, but He who is coming after me is mightier than I, and I am not fit to remove His sandals; He will baptize you with the Holy Spirit and fire (Matthew 3:11).

After being baptized, Jesus came up immediately from the water; and behold, the heavens were opened, and he saw the Spirit of God descending as a dove and lighting on Him (Matthew 3:16).

I baptized you with water; but He will baptize you with the Holy Spirit (Mark 1:8).

When Elizabeth heard Mary's greeting, the baby leaped in her womb; and Elizabeth was filled with the Holy Spirit (Luke 1:41).

And his father Zacharias was filled with the Holy Spirit, and prophesied... (Luke 1:67).

And there was a man in Jerusalem whose name was Simeon; and this man was righteous and devout, looking for the consolation of Israel; and the Holy Spirit was upon him (Luke 2:25).

John answered and said to them all, "As for me, I baptize you with water; but One is coming who is mightier than I, and I am not fit to untie the thong of His sandals; He will baptize you with the Holy Spirit and fire (Luke 3:16).

And the Holy Spirit descended upon Him in bodily form like a dove, and a voice came out of heaven, "You are My beloved Son, in You I am well-pleased" (Luke 3:22).

Jesus, full of the Holy Spirit, returned from the Jordan and was led around by the Spirit in the wilderness (Luke 4:1).

I did not recognize Him, but He who sent me to baptize in water said to me, "He upon whom you see the Spirit descending and remaining upon Him, this is the One who baptizes in the Holy Spirit" (John 1:33).

For John baptized with water, but you will be baptized with the Holy Spirit not many days from now (Acts 1:5).

And they were all filled with the Holy Spirit and began to speak with other tongues, as the Spirit was giving them utterance (Acts 2:4).

"And it shall be in the last days," God says, "that I will pour forth My Spirit on all mankind; and your sons and daughters shall prophesy, and your young men shall see visions, and your old men shall dream dreams" (Acts 2:17).

Therefore having been exalted to the right hand of God, and having received from the Father the promise of the Holy Spirit, He has poured forth this which you both see and hear (Acts 2:33).

Then Peter, filled with the Holy Spirit, said to them... (Acts 4:8).

And when they had prayed, the place where they had gathered together was shaken, and they were all filled with the Holy Spirit and began to speak the word of God with boldness (Acts 4:31).

The statement found approval with the whole congregation; and they chose Stephen, a man full of faith and of the Holy Spirit, and Philip, Prochorus, Nicanor, Timon, Parmenas and Nicolas, a proselyte from Antioch (Acts 6:5).

But being full of the Holy Spirit, he gazed intently into heaven and saw the glory of God, and Jesus standing at the right hand of God (Acts 7:55).

You know of Jesus of Nazareth, how God anointed Him with the Holy Spirit and with power, and how He went about doing good and healing all who were oppressed by the devil, for God was with Him (Acts 10:38).

While Peter was still speaking these words, the Holy Spirit fell upon all those who were listening to the message (Acts 10:44).

All the circumcised believers who came with Peter were amazed, because the gift of the Holy Spirit had been poured out on the Gentiles also (Acts 10:45).

And as I began to speak, the Holy Spirit fell upon them just as He did upon us at the beginning (Acts 11:15).

And I remembered the word of the Lord, how He used to say, "John baptized with water, but you will be baptized with the Holy Spirit" (Acts 11:16).

For he was a good man, and full of the Holy Spirit and of faith. And considerable numbers were brought to the Lord (Acts 11:24).

But Saul, who was also known as Paul, filled with the Holy Spirit, fixed his gaze on him (Acts 13:9).

And the disciples were continually filled with joy and with the Holy Spirit (Acts 13:52).

He said to them, "Did you receive the Holy Spirit when you believed?" And they said to him, "No, we have not even heard whether there is a Holy Spirit" (Acts 19:2).

And when Paul had laid his hands upon them, the Holy Spirit came on them, and they began speaking with tongues and prophesying (Acts 19:6).

Now may the God of hope fill you with all joy and peace in believing, so that you will abound in hope by the power of the Holy Spirit (Romans 15:13).

And do not get drunk with wine, for that is dissipation, but be filled with the Spirit (Ephesians 5:18).

Spirit of Hope

Now may the God of hope fill you with all joy and peace in believing, so that you will abound in hope by the power of the Holy Spirit (Romans 15:13).

Spirit of Prophecy

Then the Spirit of the Lord will come upon you mightily, and you shall prophesy with them and be changed into another man (1 Samuel 10:6).

When they came to the hill there, behold, a group of prophets met him; and the Spirit of God came upon him mightily, so that he prophesied among them (1 Samuel 10:10).

Then Saul sent messengers to take David, but when they saw the company of the prophets prophesying, with Samuel standing and presiding over them, the Spirit of God came upon the messengers of Saul; and they also prophesied (1 Samuel 19:20).

He proceeded there to Naioth in Ramah; and the Spirit of God came upon him also, so that he went along prophesying continually until he came to Naioth in Ramah (1 Samuel 19:23).

The Spirit of the Lord spoke by me, and His word was on my tongue (2 Samuel 23:2).

However, You bore with them for many years, and admonished them by Your Spirit through Your prophets, yet they would not give ear. Therefore You gave them into the hand of the peoples of the lands (Nehemiah 9:30).

And his father Zacharias was filled with the Holy Spirit, and prophesied... (Luke 1:67).

Brethren, the Scripture had to be fulfilled, which the Holy Spirit foretold by the mouth of David concerning Judas, who became a guide to those who arrested Jesus (Acts 1:16).

"And it shall be in the last days," God says, "that I will pour forth of My Spirit on all mankind; and your sons and your daughters shall prophesy, and your young men shall see visions, and your old men shall dream dreams" (Acts 2:17).

Even on My bondslaves, both men and women, I will in those days pour forth of My Spirit and they shall prophesy (Acts 2:18).

One of them named Agabus stood up and began to indicate by the Spirit that there would certainly be a great famine all over the world. And this took place in the reign of Claudius (Acts 11:28).

And when Paul had laid his hands upon them, the Holy Spirit came on them, and they began speaking with tongues and prophesying (Acts 19:6).

And when they did not agree with one another, they began leaving after Paul had spoken one parting word, "The Holy Spirit rightly spoke through Isaiah the prophet to your fathers" (Acts 28:25).

For no prophecy was ever made by an act of human will, but men moved by the Holy Spirit spoke from God (2 Peter 1:21).

And he carried me away in the Spirit into a wilderness; and I saw a woman sitting on a scarlet beast, full of blasphemous names, having seven heads and ten horns (Revelation 17:3).

And he carried me away in the Spirit to a great and high mountain, and showed me the holy city, Jerusalem, coming down out of heaven from God (Revelation 21:10).

Spirit of War

The Spirit of the Lord came upon him, and he judged Israel. When he went out to war, the Lord gave Cushan-rishathaim king of Mesopotamia into his hand, so that he prevailed over Cushan-rishathaim (Judges 3:10).

Then the Spirit of the Lord came upon him mightily, and he went down to Ashkelon and killed thirty of them and took their spoil and gave the changes of clothes to those who told the riddle. And his anger burned, and he went up to his father's house (Judges 14:19).

Then the Spirit of God came upon Saul mightily when he heard these words, and he became very angry (1 Samuel 11:6).

Thus says the Lord: "Behold, I am going to arouse against Babylon and against the inhabitants of Leb-kamai the spirit of a destroyer" (Jeremiah 51:1).

You know of Jesus of Nazareth, how God anointed Him with the Holy Spirit and with power, and how He went about doing good and healing all who were oppressed by the devil, for God was with Him (Acts 10:38).

Spirit of Power

Now the Spirit of the Lord came upon Jephthah, so that he passed through Gilead and Manasseh; then he passed through Mizpah of Gilead, and from Mizpah of Gilead he went on to the sons of Ammon (Judges 11:29).

The Spirit of the Lord came upon him mightily, so that he tore him as one tears a young goat though he had nothing in his hand; but he did not tell his father or mother what he had done (Judges 14:6).

It will come about when I leave you that the Spirit of the Lord will carry you where I do not know; so when I come and tell Ahab and he cannot find you, he will kill me, although I your servant have feared the Lord from my youth (1 Kings 18:12).

When he came to Lehi, the Philistines shouted as they met him. And the Spirit of the Lord came upon him mightily so that the ropes that were on his arms were as flax that is burned with fire, and his bonds dropped from his hands (Judges 15:14).

They said to him, "Behold now, there are with your servants fifty strong men, please let them go and search for your master; perhaps the Spirit of the Lord has taken him up and cast him on some mountain or into some valley." And he said, "You shall not send" (2 Kings 2:16).

The Spirit of the Lord will rest on Him…the spirit of counsel and strength… (Isaiah 11:2).

A spirit of justice for him who sits in judgment, a strength to those who repel the onslaught at the gate (Isaiah 28:6).

The Spirit of the Lord God is upon me, because the Lord has anointed me to bring good news to the afflicted; He has sent me to bind up the brokenhearted, to proclaim liberty to captives and freedom to prisoners (Isaiah 61:1).

Then the Spirit lifted me up, and I heard a great rumbling sound behind me, "Blessed be the glory of the Lord in His place" (Ezekiel 3:12).

So the Spirit lifted me up and took me away; and I went embittered in the rage of my spirit, and the hand of the Lord was strong on me (Ezekiel 3:14).

The Spirit then entered me and made me stand on my feet, and He spoke with me and said to me, "Go, shut yourself up in your house" (Ezekiel 3:24).

He stretched out the form of a hand and caught me by a lock of my head; and the Spirit lifted me up between earth and heaven and brought me in the visions of God to Jerusalem, to the entrance of the north gate of the inner court, where the seat of the idol of jealousy, which provokes to jealousy, was located (Ezekiel 8:3).

Moreover, the Spirit lifted me up and brought me to the east gate of the Lord's house which faced eastward. And behold, there were twenty-five men at the entrance of the gate, and among them I saw Jaazaniah son of Azzur and Pelatiah son of Benaiah, leaders of the people (Ezekiel 11:1).

Then the Spirit of the Lord fell upon me, and He said to me, "Say, 'Thus says the Lord, "So you think, house of Israel, for I know your thoughts"'" (Ezekiel 11:5).

And the Spirit lifted me up and brought me in a vision by the Spirit of God to the exiles in Chaldea. So the vision that I had seen left me (Ezekiel 11:24).

The hand of the Lord was upon me, and He brought me out by the Spirit of the Lord and set me down in the middle of the valley; and it was full of bones (Ezekiel 37:1).

And the Spirit lifted me up and brought me into the inner court; and behold, the glory of the Lord filled the house (Ezekiel 43:5).

On the other hand I am filled with power—with the Spirit of the Lord—and with justice and courage to make known to Jacob his rebellious act, even to Israel his sin (Micah 3:8).

For he will be great in the sight of the Lord; and he will drink no wine or liquor, and he will be filled with the Holy Spirit while yet in his mother's womb (Luke 1:15).

And Jesus returned to Galilee in the power of the Spirit, and news about Him spread through all the surrounding district (Luke 4:14).

Until the day when He was taken up to heaven, after He had by the Holy Spirit given orders to the apostles whom He had chosen (Acts 1:2).

"And it shall be in the last days," God says, "that I will pour forth of My Spirit on all mankind; and your sons and your daughters shall prophesy, and your young men shall see visions, and your old men shall dream dreams" (Acts 2:17).

Who by the Holy Spirit, through the mouth of our father David Your servant, said, "Why did the Gentiles rage, and the peoples devise futile things?" (Acts 4:25).

When they came up out of the water, the Spirit of the Lord snatched Philip away; and the eunuch no longer saw him, but went on his way rejoicing (Acts 8:39).

So Ananias departed and entered the house, and after laying his hands on him said, "Brother Saul, the Lord Jesus, who appeared to you on the road by which you were coming, has sent me so that you may regain your sight and be filled with the Holy Spirit" (Acts 9:17).

You know of Jesus of Nazareth, how God anointed Him with the Holy Spirit and with power, and how He went about doing good and healing all who were oppressed by the devil, for God was with Him (Acts 10:38).

Now after these things were finished, Paul purposed in the Spirit to go to Jerusalem after he had passed through Macedonia and Achaia, saying, "After I have been there, I must also see Rome" (Acts 19:21).

Now may the God of hope fill you with all joy and peace in believing, so that you will abound in hope by the power of the Holy Spirit (Romans 15:13).

In the power of signs and wonders, in the power of the Spirit; so that from Jerusalem and round about as far as Illyricum I have fully preached the gospel of Christ (Romans 15:19).

And my message and my preaching were not in persuasive words of wisdom, but in demonstration of the Spirit and of power (1 Corinthians 2:4).

So then, does He who provides you with the Spirit and works miracles among you, do it by the works of the Law, or by hearing with faith? (Galatians 3:5).

That He would grant you, according to the riches of His glory, to be strengthened with power through His Spirit in the inner man (Ephesians 3:16).

For our gospel did not come to you in word only, but also in power and in the Holy Spirit and with full conviction; just as you know what kind of men we proved to be among you for your sake (1 Thessalonians 1:5).

I was in the Spirit on the Lord's day, and I heard behind me a loud voice like the sound of a trumpet (Revelation 1:10).

Immediately I was in the Spirit; and behold, a throne was standing in heaven, and One sitting on the throne (Revelation 4:2).

And he carried me away in the Spirit to a great and high mountain, and showed me the holy city, Jerusalem, coming down out of heaven from God (Revelation 21:10).

The Spirit and the bride say, "Come." And let the one who hears say, "Come." And let the one who is thirsty come; let the one who wishes take the water of life without cost (Revelation 22:17).

Breath of God

As He spoke to me the Spirit entered me and set me on my feet; and I heard Him speaking to me (Ezekiel 2:2).

Spirit of Love

Seek from the book of the Lord, and read: Not one of these will be missing; none will lack its mate. For His mouth has commanded, and His Spirit has gathered them (Isaiah 34:16).

David himself said in the Holy Spirit, "The Lord said to my Lord, 'Sit at My right hand, until I put Your enemies beneath Your feet'" (Mark 12:36).

For it seemed good to the Holy Spirit and to us to lay upon you no greater burden than these essentials (Acts 15:28).

And hope does not disappoint, because the love of God has been poured out within our hearts through the Holy Spirit who was given to us (Romans 5:5).

Now I urge you, brethren, by our Lord Jesus Christ and by the love of the Spirit, to strive together with me in your prayers to God for me (Romans 15:30).

But the one who joins himself to the Lord is one spirit with Him (1 Corinthians 6:17).

In purity, in knowledge, in patience, in kindness, in the Holy Spirit, in genuine love (2 Corinthians 6:6).

The grace of the Lord Jesus Christ, and the love of God, and the fellowship of the Holy Spirit, be with you all (2 Corinthians 13:14).

But the fruit of the Spirit is love, joy, peace, patience, kindness, goodness, faithfulness (Galatians 5:22).

Being diligent to preserve the unity of the Spirit in the bond of peace (Ephesians 4:3).

Therefore if there is any encouragement in Christ, if there is any consolation of love, if there is any fellowship of the Spirit, if any affection and compassion (Philippians 2:1).

And he also informed us of your love in the Spirit (Colossians 1:8).

Or do you think that the Scripture speaks to no purpose: "He jealously desires the Spirit which He has made to dwell in us"? (James 4:5).

These are the ones who cause divisions, worldly-minded, devoid of the Spirit (Jude 1:19).

Spirit of Faith

For he was a good man, and full of the Holy Spirit and of faith. And considerable numbers were brought to the Lord (Acts 11:24).

Now may the God of hope fill you with all joy and peace in believing, so that you will abound in hope by the power of the Holy Spirit (Romans 15:13).

To another faith by the same Spirit, and to another gifts of healing by the one Spirit (1 Corinthians 12:9).

But having the same spirit of faith, according to what is written, "I believed, therefore I spoke," we also believe, therefore we also speak (2 Corinthians 4:13).

This is the only thing I want to find out from you: did you receive the Spirit by the works of the Law, or by hearing with faith? (Galatians 3:2).

So then, does He who provides you with the Spirit and works miracles among you, do it by the works of the Law, or by hearing with faith? (Galatians 3:5).

But the fruit of the Spirit is love, joy, peace, patience, kindness, goodness, faithfulness (Galatians 5:22).

Spirit of the Fear of the Lord

The Spirit of the Lord will rest on Him, the spirit of wisdom and understanding, the spirit of counsel and strength, the spirit of knowledge and the fear of the Lord (Isaiah 11:2).

So the church throughout all Judea and Galilee and Samaria enjoyed peace, being built up; and going on in the fear of the Lord and in the comfort of the Holy Spirit, it continued to increase (Acts 9:31).

Spirit Who Is Grieved

Now the Spirit of the Lord departed from Saul, and an evil spirit from the Lord terrorized him (1 Samuel 16:14).

But they rebelled and grieved His Holy Spirit; therefore He turned Himself to become their enemy, He fought against them (Isaiah 63:10).

You men who are stiff-necked and uncircumcised in heart and ears are always resisting the Holy Spirit; you are doing just as your fathers did (Acts 7:51).

Do not grieve the Holy Spirit of God, by whom you were sealed for the day of redemption (Ephesians 4:30).

Spirit of the Lord

Because they were rebellious against His Spirit, he spoke rashly with his lips (Psalm 106:33).

The Spirit of the Lord will rest on Him, the spirit of wisdom and understanding, the spirit of counsel and strength, the spirit of knowledge and the fear of the Lord (Isaiah 11:2).

"Woe to the rebellious children," declares the Lord, "who execute a plan, but not Mine, and make an alliance, but not of My Spirit, in order to add sin to sin" (Isaiah 30:1).

Who has directed the Spirit of the Lord, or as His counselor has informed Him? (Isaiah 40:13).

The Spirit of the Lord God is upon me, because the Lord has anointed me to bring good news to the afflicted; He has sent me to bind up the brokenhearted, to proclaim liberty to captives and freedom to prisoners (Isaiah 61:1).

As the cattle which go down into the valley, the Spirit of the Lord gave them rest. So You led Your people, to make for Yourself a glorious name (Isaiah 63:14).

And each went straight forward; wherever the spirit was about to go, they would go, without turning as they went (Ezekiel 1:12).

While they were ministering to the Lord and fasting, the Holy Spirit said, "Set apart for Me Barnabas and Saul for the work to which I have called them" (Acts 13:2).

So, being sent out by the Holy Spirit, they went down to Seleucia and from there they sailed to Cyprus (Acts 13:4).

And now, behold, bound by the Spirit, I am on my way to Jerusalem, not knowing what will happen to me there (Acts 20:22).

Be on guard for yourselves and for all the flock, among which the Holy Spirit has made you overseers, to shepherd the church of God which He purchased with His own blood (Acts 20:28).

Present Spirit

Where can I go from Your Spirit? Or where can I flee from Your presence? (Psalm 139:7).

Then His people remembered the days of old, of Moses. Where is He who brought them up out of the sea with the shepherds of His flock? Where is He who put His Holy Spirit in the midst of them (Isaiah 63:11)

As for the promise which I made you when you came out of Egypt, My Spirit is abiding in your midst; do not fear! (Haggai 2:5).

When they arrest you and hand you over, do not worry before-hand about what you are to say, but say whatever is given you in that hour; for it is not you who speak, but it is the Holy Spirit (Mark 13:11).

Good Spirit

Teach me to do Your will, for You are my God; let Your good Spirit lead me on level ground (Psalm 143:10).

Is it being said, O house of Jacob: "Is the Spirit of the Lord impatient? Are these His doings?" Do not My words do good to the one walking uprightly? (Micah 2:7).

But to each one is given the manifestation of the Spirit for the common good (1 Corinthians 12:7).

Indwelling Spirit

The spirit of man is the lamp of the Lord, searching all the innermost parts of his being (Proverbs 20:27).

I am telling the truth in Christ, I am not lying, my conscience testifies with me in the Holy Spirit (Romans 9:1).

Do you not know that you are a temple of God and that the Spirit of God dwells in you? (1 Corinthians 3:16).

Or do you not know that your body is a temple of the Holy Spirit who is in you, whom you have from God, and that you are not your own? (1 Corinthians 6:19).

Who also sealed us and gave us the Spirit in our hearts as a pledge (2 Corinthians 1:22).

That He would grant you, according to the riches of His glory, to be strengthened with power through His Spirit in the inner man (Ephesians 3:16).

The grace of the Lord Jesus Christ be with your spirit (Philemon 1:25).

Spirit of Judgment

When the Lord has washed away the filth of the daughters of Zion and purged the bloodshed of Jerusalem from her midst, by the spirit of judgment and the spirit of burning (Isaiah 4:4).

Spirit of Peace

For the kingdom of God is not eating and drinking, but righteousness and peace and joy in the Holy Spirit (Romans 14:17).

Now may the God of hope fill you with all joy and peace in believing, so that you will abound in hope by the power of the Holy Spirit (Romans 15:13).

But the fruit of the Spirit is love, joy, peace, patience, kindness, goodness, faithfulness (Galatians 5:22).

Being diligent to preserve the unity of the Spirit in the bond of peace (Ephesians 4:3).

Spirit of Fire

When the Lord has washed away the filth of the daughters of Zion and purged the bloodshed of Jerusalem from her midst, by the spirit of judgment and the spirit of burning (Isaiah 4:4).

Saving Spirit

Behold, My Servant, whom I uphold; My chosen one in whom My soul delights. I have put My Spirit upon Him; He will bring forth justice to the nations (Isaiah 42:1).

The Spirit of the Lord God is upon me, because the Lord has anointed me to bring good news to the afflicted; He has sent me to bind up the brokenhearted, to proclaim liberty to captives and freedom to prisoners (Isaiah 61:1).

As He spoke to me the Spirit entered me and set me on my feet; and I heard Him speaking to me (Ezekiel 2:2).

Behold, My Servant whom I have chosen; My Beloved in whom My soul is well-pleased; I will put My Spirit upon Him, and He shall proclaim justice to the Gentiles (Matthew 12:18).

For he was a good man, and full of the Holy Spirit and of faith. And considerable numbers were brought to the Lord (Acts 11:24).

For the kingdom of God is not eating and drinking, but righteousness and peace and joy in the Holy Spirit (Romans 14:17).

To be a minister of Christ Jesus to the Gentiles, ministering as a priest the gospel of God, so that my offering of the Gentiles may become acceptable, sanctified by the Holy Spirit (Romans 15:16).

Therefore I make known to you that no one speaking by the Spirit of God says, "Jesus is accursed"; and no one can say, "Jesus is Lord," except by the Holy Spirit (1 Corinthians 12:3).

Who also sealed us and gave us the Spirit in our hearts as a pledge (2 Corinthians 1:22).

Now He who prepared us for this very purpose is God, who gave to us the Spirit as a pledge (2 Corinthians 5:5).

For through Him we both have our access in one Spirit to the Father (Ephesians 2:18).

But we should always give thanks to God for you, brethren beloved by the Lord, because God has chosen you from the beginning for salvation through sanctification by the Spirit and faith in the truth (2 Thessalonians 2:13).

How much more will the blood of Christ, who through the eternal Spirit offered Himself without blemish to God, cleanse your conscience from dead works to serve the living God? (Hebrews 9:14).

According to the foreknowledge of God the Father, by the sanctifying work of the Spirit, to obey Jesus Christ and be sprinkled with His blood: May grace and peace be yours in the fullest measure (1 Peter 1:2).

It was revealed to them that they were not serving themselves, but you, in these things which now have been announced to you through those who preached the gospel to you by the Holy Spirit sent from heaven—things into which angels long to look (1 Peter 1:12).

The Spirit and the water and the blood; and the three are in agreement (1 John 5:8).

Spirit of Healing

The Spirit of the Lord God is upon me, because the Lord has anointed me to bring good news to the afflicted; He has sent me to bind up the brokenhearted, to proclaim liberty to captives and freedom to prisoners (Isaiah 61:1).

As He spoke to me the Spirit entered me and set me on my feet; and I heard Him speaking to me (Ezekiel 2:2).

So Ananias departed and entered the house, and after laying his hands on him said, "Brother Saul, the Lord Jesus, who appeared to you on the road by which you were coming, has sent me so that you may regain your sight and be filled with the Holy Spirit" (Acts 9:17).

You know of Jesus of Nazareth, how God anointed Him with the Holy Spirit and with power, and how He went about doing good and healing all who were oppressed by the devil, for God was with Him (Acts 10:38).

To another faith by the same Spirit, and to another gifts of healing by the one Spirit (1 Corinthians 12:9).

So then, does He who provides you with the Spirit and works miracles among you, do it by the works of the Law, or by hearing with faith? (Galatians 3:5).

God also testifying with them, both by signs and wonders and by various miracles and by gifts of the Holy Spirit according to His own will (Hebrews 2:4).

Spirit of Revival

For I will pour out water on the thirsty land and streams on the dry ground; I will pour out My Spirit on your offspring and My blessing on your descendants (Isaiah 44:3).

I will not hide My face from them any longer, for I will have poured out My Spirit on the house of Israel," declares the Lord God (Ezekiel 39:29).

It will come about after this that I will pour out My Spirit on all mankind; and your sons and daughters will prophesy, your old men will dream dreams, your young men will see visions (Joel 2:28).

Even on the male and female servants I will pour out My Spirit in those days (Joel 2:29).

Spirit of the King

But if I cast out demons by the Spirit of God, then the kingdom of God has come upon you (Matthew 12:28).

For the kingdom of God is not eating and drinking, but righteousness and peace and joy in the Holy Spirit (Romans 14:17).

Spirit of Rest

As the cattle which go down into the valley, the Spirit of the Lord gave them rest. So You led Your people, to make for Yourself a glorious name (Isaiah 63:14).

And I heard a voice from heaven, saying, "Write, 'Blessed are the dead who die in the Lord from now on!'" "Yes," says the Spirit, "so that they may rest from their labors, for their deeds follow with them" (Revelation 14:13).

Spirit of Prayer

I will pour out on the house of David and on the inhabitants of Jerusalem, the Spirit of grace and of supplication, so that they will look on Me whom they have pierced; and they will mourn for

Him, as one mourns for an only son, and they will weep bitterly over Him like the bitter weeping over a firstborn (Zechariah 12:10).

Now I urge you, brethren, by our Lord Jesus Christ and by the love of the Spirit, to strive together with me in your prayers to God for me (Romans 15:30).

For if I pray in a tongue, my spirit *prays, but my mind is unfruitful* (1 Corinthians 14:14).

What is the outcome then? I will pray with the spirit *and I will pray with the mind also; I will sing with the* spirit *and I will sing with the mind also* (1 Corinthians 14:15).

With all prayer and petition pray at all times in the Spirit, and with this in view, be on the alert with all perseverance and petition for all the saints (Ephesians 6:18).

The end of all things is near; therefore, be of sound judgment and sober spirit *for the purpose of prayer* (1 Peter 4:7).

But you, beloved, building yourselves up on your most holy faith, praying in the Holy Spirit (Jude 1:20).

Spirit and Power of Elijah

It is he who will go as a forerunner before Him in the spirit *and power of Elijah, to turn the hearts of the fathers back to the children, and the disobedient to the attitude of the righteous, so as to make ready a people prepared for the Lord* (Luke 1:17).

Spirit of Joy

And Jesus returned to Galilee in the power of the Spirit, and news about Him spread through all the surrounding district (Luke 4:14).

At that very time He rejoiced greatly in the Holy Spirit, and said, "I praise You, O Father, Lord of heaven and earth, that You have hidden these things from the wise and intelligent and have revealed them to infants. Yes, Father, for this way was well-pleasing in Your sight" (Luke 10:21).

And the disciples were continually filled with joy and with the Holy Spirit (Acts 13:52).

For the kingdom of God is not eating and drinking, but righteousness and peace and joy in the Holy Spirit (Romans 14:17).

Now may the God of hope fill you with all joy and peace in believing, so that you will abound in hope by the power of the Holy Spirit (Romans 15:13).

But the fruit of the Spirit is love, joy, peace, patience, kindness, goodness, faithfulness (Galatians 5:22).

You also became imitators of us and of the Lord, having received the word in much tribulation with the joy of the Holy Spirit (1 Thessalonians 1:6).

Do not quench the Spirit (1 Thessalonians 5:19).

Promised Spirit

If you then, being evil, know how to give good gifts to your children, how much more will your heavenly Father give the Holy Spirit to those who ask Him? (Luke 11:13).

Therefore having been exalted to the right hand of God, and having received from the Father the promise of the Holy Spirit, He has poured forth this which you both see and hear (Acts 2:33).

In order that in Christ Jesus the blessing of Abraham might come to the Gentiles, so that we would receive the promise of the Spirit through faith (Galatians 3:14).

The Gift of the Spirit

But this He spoke of the Spirit, whom those who believed in Him were to receive; for the Spirit was not yet given, because Jesus was not yet glorified (John 7:39).

For He whom God has sent speaks the words of God; for He gives the Spirit without measure (John 3:34).

Peter said to them, "Repent, and each of you be baptized in the name of Jesus Christ for the forgiveness of your sins; and you will receive the gift of the Holy Spirit" (Acts 2:38).

And we are witnesses of these things; and so is the Holy Spirit, whom God has given to those who obey Him (Acts 5:32).

Who came down and prayed for them that they might receive the Holy Spirit (Acts 8:15).

Then they began laying their hands on them, and they were receiving the Holy Spirit (Acts 8:17).

Now when Simon saw that the Spirit was bestowed through the laying on of the apostles' hands, he offered them money (Acts 8:18).

All the circumcised believers who came with Peter were amazed, because the gift of the Holy Spirit had been poured out on the Gentiles also (Acts 10:45).

Surely no one can refuse the water for these to be baptized who have received the Holy Spirit just as we did, can he? (Acts 10:47).

And God, who knows the heart, testified to them giving them the Holy Spirit, just as He also did to us (Acts 15:8).

He said to them, "Did you receive the Holy Spirit when you believed?" And they said to him, "No, we have not even heard whether there is a Holy Spirit" (Acts 19:2).

Spirit of Truth

That is the Spirit of truth, whom the world cannot receive, because it does not see Him or know Him, but you know Him because He abides with you and will be in you (John 14:17).

But when He, the Spirit of truth, comes, He will guide you into all the truth; for He will not speak on His own initiative, but whatever He hears, He will speak; and He will disclose to you what is to come (John 16:13).

We are from God; he who knows God listens to us; he who is not from God does not listen to us. By this we know the spirit *of truth and the* spirit *of error* (1 John 4:6).

This is the One who came by water and blood, Jesus Christ; not with the water only, but with the water and with the blood. It is the Spirit who testifies, because the Spirit is the truth (1 John 5:6).

Helper

But the Helper, the Holy Spirit, whom the Father will send in My name, He will teach you all things, and bring to your remembrance all that I said to you (John 14:26).

When the Helper comes, whom I will send to you from the Father, that is the Spirit of truth who proceeds from the Father, He will testify about Me (John 15:26).

While Peter was reflecting on the vision, the Spirit said to him, "Behold, three men are looking for you" (Acts 10:19).

Comforter

So the church throughout all Judea and Galilee and Samaria enjoyed peace, being built up; and going on in the fear of the Lord and in the comfort of the Holy Spirit, it continued to increase (Acts 9:31).

Gift Giver

Now there are varieties of gifts, but the same Spirit (1 Corinthians 12:4).

But to each one is given the manifestation of the Spirit for the common good (1 Corinthians 12:7).

For to one is given the word of wisdom through the Spirit, and to another the word of knowledge according to the same Spirit (1 Corinthians 12:8).

To another faith by the same Spirit, and to another gifts of healing by the one Spirit (1 Corinthians 12:9).

But one and the same Spirit works all these things, distributing to each one individually just as He wills (1 Corinthians 12:11).

God also testifying with them, both by signs and wonders and by various miracles and by gifts of the Holy Spirit according to His own will (Hebrews 2:4).

For in the case of those who have once been enlightened and have tasted of the heavenly gift and have been made partakers of the Holy Spirit (Hebrews 6:4).

Living Water

He who believes in Me, as the Scripture said, "From his innermost being will flow rivers of living water" (John 7:38).

For by one Spirit we were all baptized into one body, whether Jews or Greeks, whether slaves or free, and we were all made to drink of one Spirit (1 Corinthians 12:13).

The Spirit and the bride say, "Come." And let the one who hears say, "Come." And let the one who is thirsty come; let the one who wishes take the water of life without cost (Revelation 22:17).

Seal of the Spirit

Who also sealed us and gave us the Spirit in our hearts as a pledge (2 Corinthians 1:22).

In Him, you also, after listening to the message of truth, the gospel of your salvation—having also believed, you were sealed in Him with the Holy Spirit of promise (Ephesians 1:13).

Do not grieve the Holy Spirit of God, by whom you were sealed for the day of redemption (Ephesians 4:30).

Spirit of Glory

How will the ministry of the Spirit fail to be even more with glory? (2 Corinthians 3:8).

If you are reviled for the name of Christ, you are blessed, because the Spirit of glory and of God rests on you (1 Peter 4:14).

Spirit of Hope

For we through the Spirit, by faith, are waiting for the hope of righteousness (Galatians 5:5).

Sword of the Spirit

And take the helmet of salvation, and the sword of the Spirit, which is the word of God (Ephesians 6:17).

Spirit of Grace

How much severer punishment do you think he will deserve who has trampled under foot the Son of God, and has regarded as unclean the blood of the covenant by which he was sanctified, and has insulted the Spirit of grace? (Hebrews 10:29).

Speaking Spirit

He who has an ear, let him hear what the Spirit says to the churches. To him who overcomes, I will grant to eat of the tree of life which is in the Paradise of God (Revelation 2:7).

He who has an ear, let him hear what the Spirit says to the churches. He who overcomes will not be hurt by the second death (Revelation 2:11).

He who has an ear, let him hear what the Spirit says to the churches. To him who overcomes, to him I will give some of the hidden manna, and I will give him a white stone, and a new name written on the stone which no one knows but he who receives it (Revelation 2:17).

He who has an ear, let him hear what the Spirit says to the churches (Revelation 2:29; 3:6,13,22).

NOTE

1. Unless otherwise noted, the Scriptures in this chapter are taken from the New American Standard Bible.

Chapter Twenty-Three

HOLY SPIRIT STORIES

When the Holy Spirit becomes your friend and a conversation begins between you and Him, He will literally blow your mind. You will discover that He never stops working, He never stops speaking. He is constantly inviting us to be with Him. He loves to nudge us and ask us to do something to reveal the love of Jesus in the lives of others. I have found that He has an incredible sense of humor, and He will also shock us at times. One thing I'm learning as I walk with Him more closely is that He does not compartmentalize our lives. I believe the day of ministers touching people's lives on the platform alone are coming to an end. The Holy Spirit does not have an off switch, and He does not turn off when we leave a pulpit or a platform. His heart still burns for people. I would venture to say that the coming wave of evangelism that will sweep the nations of the earth will not be dominated by public ministry but by everyday people like you and me who are simply listening to the Holy Spirit as we get close to Him and obey Him.

I remember about six years ago, my good friend Eric Gilmour and I were driving to a bookstore to purchase some books written by some of the old spiritual writers of the past. We were just leaving Christ for all Nations, where we were doing some media. The car we were driving needed gas. So we pulled over into a gas station in a pretty rough neighborhood. Eric, as he always used to in those days, had a video camera with him. He would turn it on out of nowhere and point it directly into my face and ask me what God was telling me. At first, it was annoying, but then I learned to appreciate Eric's hunger for the things of God. So, there I was pumping gas, and sure enough, Eric whipped out his camera, placed it on a tripod, and put it in my face. He said, "What's God been speaking to you?" I had nothing spiritual on my mind at the time, and I thought it was funny. Instantly, out of the corner of my eye, across the parking lot of this gas station in this horrible neighborhood I saw a man walking with a shopping cart. He was clearly homeless and walked with a noticeable limp. The moment he caught my eye, I heard the Holy Spirit say, "Go and lay hands on him and pray for his ailment."

So, I left the gas nozzle in my car and immediately left my car unattended and walked over to the man who clearly had a very, very injured leg. Once we introduced ourselves, he gave us his name, which I'll never forget. It was Jack. Initially, he was very scared. He thought we were going to hurt him. Then a car full of young people from the neighborhood drove up and said, "What are you going to do to the man? Are you going to hurt him?"

We said, "No, no, we're not going to hurt him," and we chuckled to ourselves because we knew God was going to do the exact opposite of that. As we talked to him about Jesus, I put my hand on the man's hip, right there in the middle of the parking lot. As I did that, I felt something on me. Now I know it was the presence of the Spirit. I took his shopping cart and pushed it away from him. He panicked.

He said, "You don't understand—I can't walk without that cart." The man was so poor he did not have money for a walker or a cane, so that cart had become his personal mobility assistance device. Led of the Spirit, I took the cart and pushed it away from him. Now he had no cart at all. He said, "I can't walk without it."

I said, "Well, you're going to have to. Today is your day." I grabbed his hand and began to walk with him through the parking lot. And after the first few steps, I saw a tear running down his face.

He said, "You don't understand—I couldn't do this before." And then we started to walk more, and more, and more, and more, until his pace increased and the Lord had touched and healed him. His eyes were full of tears, and they streamed down his face. Then Eric sat down with him and shared the Gospel with him. I'll never forget that day, not because it was the greatest miracle I've ever seen. To be honest, I hate to rate miracles because all of them require the blood and stripes of Jesus. Since everything is valued by what somebody is willing to pay for it, every miracle is valuable because Jesus is valuable. Was it the grandest miracle I've ever seen? No. It sticks out to me because of the way that the Holy Spirit orchestrated the whole thing. We were leaving a major ministry simply to go to a bookstore and go deeper with Jesus. The car was low on gas, and the Lord knew that we would have to stop. The last place I thought I'd see miracles is at the gas pump, but the beauty of the will of the Spirit is like nothing we've ever known.

Another time, my wife and I went to downtown Orlando to grab some lunch. I believe we got a hamburger together. As I was driving through the downtown area, which is very busy with traffic, on our way home, I saw a man in a wheelchair wheeling himself down the sidewalk. I passed him and kept driving. Instantly, I felt a check in my spirit and heard the voice of the Holy Spirit. He said, "Go pray for that man." I thought to myself, "How inconvenient. I'm downtown, where there's traffic. You want me to turn around, Lord? Where will I park the car? What will I do with Jess?" The Lord said, "Just turn the car around."

So, I turned the car around and went to find him. Sure enough, he was wheeling himself down the sidewalk on the other side of the street. I crossed the street in the car and found a parking space. I parallel parked the car, looked at my wife, and said, "Jess, I'll be right back."

She said, "What are you doing?"

I said, "I'm going to pray for that man."

She said, "Okay."

I said, "You wait here in the car." So, Jessica stayed with the car. I jumped out. Between the car and the man for whom I was going to pray was a group of cars. For all my wife knew, I had just jumped out. She would have no way of knowing what the Lord would do. I walked up to the man. I said, "Sir, my name's Michael. I'm in the ministry, and I live in this area. As I was driving by you, I heard the Holy Spirit say, 'Go pray for that man.'" He started crying. I said, "Sir, why are you crying?"

He said, "I was a Baptist minister, and I failed. I had a moral failure, and I was kicked out of the ministry." It was clear this man had some addictions and many other issues in his life that God needed to heal.

So, I said, "I believe the Lord sent me to you so that He would heal you today and you would see His power and His love." As he continued to cry, I put my hand on him. I said, "Lord, I thank You for Your healing power that flows through this man. In the name of Jesus, be healed." And so, I stood him up, and he began to walk. I asked him, "When is the last time you were able to walk like this?"

He said, "It's been years." He added, "I'm not paralyzed. I have been able to stand up, but I've not been able to do what I'm doing right now for years." He continued to cry. It was a full-blown healing right there on the street.

Now, Jessica was still in the car. She had been on a phone call while I was out praying for the man. Once I got in the car, I put the car in drive, and we drove off. Because she was on the phone I couldn't share the testimony with her right away. So, we took a right at the stop sign and began to drive home. Jessica looked to her right, and instead of seeing a man wheeling himself down the road, she saw the same man walking all by himself. She got off the phone and said, "Oh my, wait! Is that the man? Wait—is that the man in the wheelchair? He's walking."

I looked at her and smiled. I could sense the pleasure and humor of the Lord. This is what the Holy Spirit does. This is His way. He is the master of these types of situations.

A friend of mine named Dave Popovici, who is now a missionary in northern Iraq, invited me to preach at his church in Chicago. When I went to the church, I began to teach on the presence of Jesus. I could sense the power of God as I was speaking. The people were hungry; they were gripped. There was a strong group of young people there who were part of the FIRE School of Ministry. I sensed a deep connection with the hearts in this church and movement. When I was through preaching, as I usually do I went back into worship. As we began to worship the Lord, I felt His power come upon me. There is no denying the power of the Holy Spirit when it begins to flow. Sometimes I feel tingling all over my body. Sometimes I feel electricity flowing through my hands. Sometimes my hands feel like they each weigh twenty pounds. Sometimes my entire body is flooded with life and joy.

A young girl grabbed my attention. She was standing there with her mother, and she was about five years old at the time. I noticed she had huge Coke-bottle glasses on. She was a precious little girl with a very sweet spirit. I walked up to her, took off her glasses, and I prayed for her eyes. The power of God hit her, and I walked away to pray for others. It was an awesome meeting, but I never got a testimony from the little girl or her mother.

Five years later, I was preaching across the country near Sacramento, California, in a conference that our friend Erica Mahea was hosting. As I began to minister, that same power began to flow again. This time, people were healed of multiple issues, and they began to fall under the power of God. It really was a glorious meeting. I noticed a young mother with a daughter who seemed to be twelve or thirteen years old. They walked up to me, but while they looked a bit familiar, I could not place their faces. The mother said, "I have a testimony to share with you and this whole church." So, I gave her the microphone. She said, "Five years ago, Michael came to my church in Chicago. He walked up to my daughter, put his hand on her, and prayed that God would give her her vision back. The power of God swept through my daughter, and that night her eyes were completely healed. In fact, when she put her Coke-bottle glasses on, everything was blurry and she could not see. I just want to share this testimony with all of you so that you can see what God did in that meeting with Michael." I was shocked to my core. Maybe you're asking, "Well, should you be shocked? Shouldn't you expect miracles?" Yes, we should expect them, but they still shock us. They're incredible. We're to be like little children, enjoying the Father's love and power and being blown away by His wonder.

You have to understand, I'm the first to realize that I do not deserve to see these things. When I do see them, I am in awe of God. The lady continued to share the testimony of her daughter—that she had been completely healed and made whole and that since that day, she had begun to encounter God in a beautiful way. The Holy Spirit is the master healer, and you can trust Him to use your life in the same way.

You'll notice I'm sharing stories with you. It's important we understand that life in the Holy Spirit is not a concept but a lived experience. He's not a topic, but a person. He's not a subject, but an individual who longs to live with us, and among us, and in us.

Our family loves to visit Winter Park, Florida. It's about twenty minutes from our home. It's a beautiful downtown district with cobblestone streets and stunning aged oak trees. The buildings are classical. The shopping is great, and so is the food. One day, we went down to Winter Park with our family to have some lunch and get the kids dessert. They love ice cream. When we were through at the ice cream shop, I walked outside the store and looked to my left. There was an elderly woman sitting on a bench. I grabbed my kids and said, "Guys, come watch this." You see, I want my children to know how simple it is to walk with the Holy Spirit and how He brings the love of Jesus much more clearly and beautifully than we ever could in our own strength. I also want them to see the fruit of obedience. Some of us believe that if we don't see the miracle, we failed. No, we have to teach our children to celebrate taking risks. So, I walked up to this woman, sat down on the bench next to her with my children and my brother-in-law Josh, and I said, "Ma'am, my name is Michael. I'm a minister here in the area. The Lord sent me to you."

She said, "Really?"

I said, "Yes, He did. Do you have any pain in your body?"

"I do, actually," she replied.

I asked, "Do you mind if I lay hands on you and pray for you?"

She said, "No, I don't mind. Please do."

So, I put my hand on her, and I told my children, "Guys, come over here. You pray for her too." And so, they began to pray for this dear woman, and she became very emotional. I said, "Ma'am, has the pain left your body?"

"It has! It has!" She exclaimed, "Who are you?"

I just said, "Just somebody who is following Jesus." My kids were blown away that God would use them in that way. I remember my brother-in-law asking, "Dude, does that happen everywhere you go?" How I wish it did! But it is happening more and more and more as I learn to listen to and obey the voice of the Holy Spirit.

One evening, we were in a large crusade with my father-in-law. In those days, I would learn the voice of the Spirit by walking through the crowd and asking Him who He was healing. I learned it was more effective to join what God was doing and agree with the people that He was already touching in the crowd. That is not the only way to see miracles, but since we were under a time restraint, the Holy Spirit began to show me this way of seeing breakthrough for those who are suffering. As I walked through the crowd, I noticed that my wife was speaking to a lady. There were people gathered around her in a huge circle, not to mention an entire section of people above her looking down. It was quite a scene. Jessica saw me and called me over to her.

She said, "My husband can open your ears." And I thought to myself, "What? What kind of pressure is this? Besides, I'm not the healer. I can't open any ears on my best day." Well, I knew what Jess meant, but it still put a lot of pressure on me and at the time was something for which I was not ready. There was a huge crowd standing around us in a circle with a deaf person standing in the middle. Beyond that, as I said, an entire section of the church was above us looking down. I prayed for the woman. I put my finger in her ear and commanded her ears to open. I was very nervous. Nothing happened when I prayed.

I asked, "Can you hear?"

"No," she replied.

I tried again. Nothing happened. At this point, I was so embarrassed. Here I was, called out and in a stadium with people watching. I'm in the ministry, and I can't get these ears to open. So, I tried again—nothing happened. For some reason, something deep in my soul said, "Just don't give up. Keep going." I tried a fourth time. I said, "Ma'am, can you hear?"

"No," she said.

I tried a fifth time. "Open, in Jesus' name!" Nothing.

A sixth time—nothing happened. It was the seventh time, I believe, that I just stayed with it and said, "In Jesus' name, open!"

I will never forget the look on this woman's face when my mouth uttered the word "open." Her eyes got huge. The smile was all consuming. Excitement was beaming out of her face, and she began to scream, "They're open! I can hear! I can hear!"

Can you imagine the first thing you can hear being a stadium full of people worshiping Jesus? Well, I was as emotional as she was. For the life of me, I couldn't believe it. What a lesson the Holy Spirit taught me—that He empowers us when we step out. He empowers those who take risks. He energizes the moments of those who put their reputations aside and are willing to look foolish for His glory.

Life with the Holy Spirit might be many things, but, my friend, I can assure you that it is far from boring. Yes, He will challenge you. Yes, He will take you to the end of yourself with His spoken word, wanting you to obey. But He always has something up His sleeve that we can't see. He always has something better than we can ever imagine waiting for us on the other end. The Scripture says, "No eye has seen, no ear has heard, no mind conceived what God has in store for those who love Him" (see 1 Cor. 2:9). The stories I just shared with you are only a few of the many I have seen around the world and at home. I'd like to share another one with you, if that's okay, because many people believe that these miracles only happen overseas or in stadiums.

One evening, in Baldwin Park, Florida, where my brother Theo was pastoring at the time, I was asked to lead a Bible study in a very young church plant that he and his wife, Rachel, were orchestrating. It was a very small group of maybe eight people. We sat in a circle with our Bibles open, and I began to teach the Scriptures. A woman walked in off the street. It was pretty clear that she did not know the Lord and she was searching for help. She came in and said, "I just left the ER, where my daughter is because she tried to kill herself by taking pills. She did not die, but she almost did." It was clear that the mother was very distraught and sad. So, she came seeking help and peace. As she began to share the horrific details of what she and her daughter were going through, she also shared with me that her husband had left her. Now she was all alone with a daughter trying to commit suicide. She was on her way back to her house, which was just across the street from where we were hosting the Bible study, and she decided to come in.

As she sat there crying, some would say, "This is not a Bible study. This woman has interrupted our 'discipleship' time." It's important we understand that Jesus never called us to disciple out of His presence. In our Western theory, we believe that discipleship belongs in a classroom with a dry erase board, but when Jesus called Matthew to be His disciple, He said, "Come and follow Me" (see Matt. 4:19). To the Lord, discipleship is living with Him, being around Him, hearing His voice, us speaking to Him, Him answering our questions, and Him throwing us into situations where His life has to pour through us.

The woman began to share her pain. She looked at me and said, "I have this huge goiter—this growth on my neck. Do you think God could heal it? Would you pray for me?" Very simply, by faith, I felt the presence of the Holy Spirit, and I put my hand on her neck. I would say it was about the size of a tangerine. Until the day I die, I will never forget what I felt under my hand when we simply obeyed the Holy Spirit and spoke the name of Jesus. I felt a pop, and I felt something under my hand change. It was like something disappeared. When I looked for the growth again, it was completely gone. I was blown away—so was she, and so were the people sitting around us. You talk about discipleship! This was the best stuff. She began to touch her neck over and over again. "Where is it? Oh my gosh, it's gone. Where is it? Where is it? Where is it? It's gone!" We all began to celebrate God's goodness, and I'll never forget driving home that night. I saw her walking to her house, and she was still feeling for the growth that was gone.

I want to challenge you today: Give God permission to shock you. Give God permission to mess up your schedule. Between point A and point B today, give God permission to ask you to stop for somebody. When He speaks, simply obey like a little child, and remember that you're not the healer; Jesus is. God is not looking for you to work a great miracle. He simply is looking for you to obey Him and to leave the rest to Him. I hope you'll enjoy the Holy Spirit today like you never have before.

About the Author

Michael Koulianos is an international speaker, evangelist, and founder of Jesus Image, a global ministry focused on bringing the saving and healing message of Jesus to the world. For three years, Michael served as a pastor in Southern California. He also spent seven years assisting in world missions and crusades around the globe. He is author of *The Jesus Book* and the *Jesus 365* devotional, host of the popular Jesus Conferences, and is driven to make the Son of God famous throughout the nations. Michael and his wife, Jessica, are the hosts of Jesus Image TV. They reside in Lake Mary, Florida, with their children.